FROM THE
FOSTER HOUSE
TO THE
WHITE HOUSE

TERRENCE K. WILLIAMS

FREILING

PUBLISHING

Writing and Editorial by Christen M. Jeschke

Published by Freiling Publishing, a division of Freiling Agency, LLC.

P.O. Box 1264,
Warrenton, VA 20188

www.FreilingPublishing.com

ISBN 978-1-950948-26-0

Printed in the United States of America

Table of Contents

Preface
The American Dream Is Real. 1

Chapter One
A Hard Life Is Still a Valuable Life 7

Chapter Two
Shaped by Starvation. 21

Chapter Three
Standing Up to Bullies. 33

Chapter Four
Yo-Yo Kids. 43

Chapter Five
Fostered by the System. 49

Chapter Six
How I Found Wisdom on a Farm 59

Chapter Seven
Conflicting Feelings. 71

Chapter Eight
Speaking Out 79

Chapter Nine
Put Your Money Where Your
Motor Mouth Is. 85

Chapter Ten
Snapping Back. 93

Chapter Eleven
Adoption **101**

Chapter Twelve
Make Them Laugh **107**

Chapter Thirteen
Training Day. **117**

Chapter Fourteen
Follower. **123**

Chapter Fifteen
Protection and Purpose **133**

Chapter Sixteen
Made for More **143**

Chapter Seventeen
Going Viral **153**

Chapter Eighteen
Mentors. **167**

Chapter Nineteen
The Crash **179**

Chapter Twenty
Dreams Fulfilled **187**

Epilogue
Part of the Family **199**

Preface

The American Dream Is Real

The American Dream teaches us that paupers can become presidents and that even a boy who grew up in foster houses can be welcomed into the White House.

I spent years of my childhood in starvation, yet now I was being invited to sit and eat at the table of the president of the United States of America. I may have been so excited that I peed myself a little. Nope. I definitely didn't do that, and even if I did, there is no way that I would write it in a book. To recap: President Donald J. Trump asked me to sit at his table, and I didn't pee myself one bit.

I was born into nothing; neglected, starved, abused, and beaten. I grew up without a table to sit at, let alone food to eat, yet here I was, welcomed to the table of the most important man in our nation and his family. Regardless of your politics, this should show you something important.

If you read the statistics for children raised in foster care, they are beyond bleak. Children who have been in the foster care system are less likely to graduate from high school, to graduate from college, or to maintain consistent employment. They stand a greater chance of suffering from PTSD, struggling with addiction, coping with teen pregnancy, or ending up in prison. If they have any sort of family structure to rely on, it is usually unpredictable and unstable. These are not facts that are unknown to children in foster care; they are continuously bombarded with reminders of how futile their chances of success are.

I could have easily bought the narrative that victimhood presented. I could have believed that as a black man, growing up in the projects without parents, I needed to embrace a life of dependency on the government or the state, or even addiction. This is a narrative that is so often pushed that many people adopt it as their mantra. However, this is America, and our history as our nation teaches us that we are not victims; we are overcomers. The American Dream is real. In our country, we are not subjugated to a life of victimhood; we are given the freedom to grow and reach our fullest potential, relying on the skills and abilities that God has given us to empower us, thriving and striving for more than we can imagine.

The American Dream is an ideal that encourages all of us that we are not victims of circumstances and that our humble beginnings do not restrict or hold us back from grander and greater things. The American Dream teaches us that paupers can become presidents and that even a boy who grew up in foster houses can be welcomed into the White House. The American Dream is real. No matter where you come from, no matter how you were brought up, you have an opportunity. I am proof of that. I am living the American Dream.

Chapter One

A Hard Life Is Still a Valuable Life

Opportunity is what the American Dream is all about.

My mother had nine different children with six different fathers. We were born into hardship and poverty, but I am thankful that we were born at all. Given the circumstances that we arrived into, many would argue that our lives should have never taken place. Even my crack-addicted mother recognized that our lives had value. I am thankful to her for giving all nine of us the gift of life. Giving us life gave us opportunity. Opportunity is what the American Dream is all about.

My sister, Kiesha, was only a child herself when I became her "first baby." Not yet into double digits herself when I was born, Kiesha was practically a baby herself, yet she was tasked with tending to me. My mom was too strung out to care for anyone, including herself adequately, so my sister took on most of the mothering. I was my mother's fifth child, and my grandmother said that my dad tried not to claim me as his. I don't know if we were all born with drugs in our system, but given my mother's long-standing affair with smoking crack, it seems reasonable.

The 1990s were the height of what was termed the "crack epidemic." Cocaine was combined with baking soda to produce the more affordable and profitable substance, crack. Crack was snorted or smoked with a pipe, providing a rapid and highly addictive euphoric effect. Short-lasting, it would entice the user to smoke again and again to maintain the intense high. I don't know how my mom became hooked on this substance. I only know that chasing the high of crack clouded the desire to take care of her children.

Kiesha was used to caring for her younger siblings, but I was the first baby that she remembers as being "hers." When I came home from the hospital, she placed me by her mattress in a box that she had made up for me so she could care for me round the clock. She had cared for her younger siblings for as long as she could remember, but I was the first newborn that she oversaw from the day I came home from the hospital. A child herself, Kiesha was forced into playing the role of mother too often as my mom struggled with her addiction.

Kiesha swaddled me, clothed me, and fed me, trying to keep me soothed and caring for me as best as another child can care for an infant. She would rock me and sing to me, preventing my crying from disturbing my mom. While most girls her age were riding bikes, skipping rope, or playing house, Kiesha was busy trying to keep a real home and manage our rapidly growing family.

At that time, we were living just outside of Langston, Oklahoma, a suburb of Oklahoma City. In the 1990s, Langston had a population of fewer than 1,500 people and was primarily a black community, boasting the state's only historically black college, Langston University.

We lived in an old home in the country with my mom and dad. My siblings called my father, "Daddy Duncan," but in all honesty, he was just one in a series of men that my mom cycled through her kids' lives. The house had three bedrooms. My mom and dad shared one bedroom and split us between the other two rooms. Kiesha took care of baby Travon and me in one room while my brother, Ricky, and sister, Lanana, slept in the remaining room. We didn't have beds, so everyone slept crammed onto shared mattresses that were often soiled and soaked with milk, tears, and urine.

My mom and dad would stay up through the night smoking crack and would sleep through the day. Kiesha would watch us during the day when she wasn't at school and tend to me at night. She barely slept as she woke every few hours to feed or change me before getting up and gathering the other kids ready to walk to school. Occasionally, my mom might remember to check in on Kiesha and the baby. When she was not high, she tried to be a good mom to us, but too often, her main concern was smoking crack and going out with friends.

My mom had her babies stair-stepped back to back. There seemed to always be one newborn baby and another one on the way. When I was born, I was not the only baby that Kiesha was caring for. My brother Travon was barely older than I was. Kiesha always had a baby on each hip or one screaming to be held. I can't even begin to imagine the sacrifices that Kiesha made, doing her best to meet our needs. She always had her younger siblings climbing on her, begging for food or attention.

My sister remembers that we were always crying. We were hungry, so we wailed. Our diapers were wet, so we sobbed. We needed to be held, so we called out with our arms outstretched, waiting for Kiesha to gather us up. Exhausted, Kiesha would cry silent tears as she tended to us, juggling endless feedings, dirty diapers, and a lack of adequate supplies for anything.

Kiesha tried her best, but she was always fighting an uphill battle as we outnumbered her, and she lacked the necessities for our care. Since I was the first infant that Kiesha had cared for, basically on her own from the day I came home from the hospital, there was a steep learning curve for her. She learned how to treat the umbilical cord, tend to my circumcision, rock me to sleep, and all of the other challenges that a newborn presents. She didn't always have someone to teach her what to do, so she had to figure it out for herself.

My mom didn't even take me to my six-week pediatric appointment. She wrote a note for Kiesha and my grandmother to be able to take me. They brought me to the doctor's office together, Kiesha standing in for my mother. She tried her best to ask the necessary questions for caring for a baby, attempting to remember my weight and length so that she could report it back to my mother.

My grandmother was ashamed of my mother's lack of care for us, but she lived too far away to check on us often and was raising kids of her own. When my grandmother did check on us, she was appalled by the level of neglect that my mom showed us and let loose on my mom in a sea of scathing words. My grandmother knew my mother was heavily doing drugs and made it her business to check in on us when she could.

When I was about three months old, my grandmother stopped by our house to check on me. She walked through the dilapidated structure weaving through filth, dirty diapers, and discarded drug paraphernalia, calling "TERRENCE!" repeatedly.

I was too young to answer, but she listened for my cries.

"Where's Terrence?" my grandmother demanded sharply.

"He's in there," replied my mom. "He's in the other room."

My grandmother rushed to rescue me, horrified by the scene in front of her.

Looking up at her as if to say, "Help me, please," my tear-stained eyes begged her to intervene. She tried to lift me, to comfort me, but I was tethered to a mattress in the center of the room, bound by blankets wrapped so tightly that I was unable to move. Not a loving infant swaddle, I was bundled to suppress, the blankets cocooned so tightly that they were cutting off my circulation. Had I tried to wiggle, kick, or free my arms, it would have been in vain. I was fully restrained, the blanket cutting like ropes into my skin. My grandmother feared that I would choke on some milk and pass away where I lay.

"Don't you ever do this baby like that again! Why did you do that?" she demanded, sternly lecturing my mom.

She picked me up, wiping snot off my face and noting the sagging of an unchanged and dirty diaper. I softly whimpered as she pulled me against her chest in comfort.

"I did that so he wouldn't fall off the bed," my mom justified. "How he gonna roll when he's tied up like that?"

My grandmother chewed my mom out for this and told her that she'd better straighten up, but nothing changed. Kiesha would often return from school to find me bound in this same manner, my mom attempting to keep me from moving so she could leave me unattended for hours on end. In my mom's drug-skewed haze, she probably thought that if I were restrained, I would be unable to get hurt while she left me alone—the drugs altering her ability to make responsible decisions.

My grandmother had good reason to worry about our lack of care. Neglect was standard for my mom if we interfered with her need for drugs. I don't think that my mom saw it this way. In her mind, we had Kiesha watching out for us, so it was okay to leave us. As capable as she was, Kiesha was still just a little girl, too young to carry the responsibilities of an adult.

Sometimes, my grandmother would get home late at night after working a hard shift to hear strange shuffling sounds on her back porch. She would rush outside to investigate, met with a gaggle of hungry and wailing children as the taillights of the car of whoever drove my mother disappeared down the dark lane. My grandmother would care for us as well as she could for as many days as possible, then hunt my mother down and send us back with her.

"These are your kids, and you need to care for them," she would lecture, but time after time, my mom would deposit us at my grandmother's house. She didn't give a second thought to the fact that my grandmother still had to go to work, take care of others, and tend to her own needs. My mother's priority was scoring crack, and that clouded her view of what was truly important.

One occasion, after my grandmother had watched us for several days, she had to go back to work, so she searched for my mom. She went looking for her and finally found her in a roach-infested house, hiding under some filthy clothes.

"You get out here and see about these kids. Why are you doing that?" my grandmother demanded, ordering her out of her hiding spot.

My siblings and I were hollering and crying, needing someone to watch us while my grandmother went to work. My mom remained unmoved, our cries not spurring her to action. She hid farther under the pile of clothes, pretending not to hear my grandmother and avoiding her responsibilities.

"If you don't get out from under those dirty clothes, I am going to call the police and have this dope house raided," my grandmother threatened.

My mom finally came out and took us back, but two days later, we were on my grandmother's porch again, looking just as destitute and disheveled as before. This was our normal, but it wasn't a good normal. It was chaotic and unpredictable, but it was all we knew.

After being shuffled back and forth between my mother and grandmother, my grandmother decided to keep us for a while. She thought that it would be the safest and best option for us kids, given the unpredictable patterns that my mother set.

She took us in and tended to us the best that she could while hoping that my mom would pull herself together and decide to parent properly. Being with my grandmother took some of the pressure off Kiesha for our needs and provision, but my sister and I had developed a special bond, so I still clung to Kiesha for care. Kiesha called me her "Butt-Butt" and I happily drooled and chattered when held in her arms.

This time, my mom disappeared for months. Maybe she was in rehab; perhaps she was just using. I am not sure which it was. She just faded away. My grandmother watched us, trying to make life as normal as possible for us, even taking us to a carnival in Crescent, Oklahoma. By this time, I was crawling, seemingly ready to explore the world around me. While the other kids played at the carnival, my grandmother relaxed, enjoying the sunshine and watching the crowds of people walking by. She placed me on a blanket, and I smiled and cooed, angling for attention. Grandma would watch me wander all over the entire surface of the blanket without ever crawling off. I would stretch out my tiny baby hand to consider leaving the quilt, but as soon as it would touch the grass, I would yank it back in fear at the unknown texture. My grandmother laughed and laughed as she watched me imprison myself on the blanket.

Just as I imprisoned myself on that blanket, my mother was held captive by her addiction. She could have chosen differently, but she wanted drugs. As I hesitated to explore, seeing the opportunities that were bigger and better than the safety of my blanket, my mother chose the comfort of drugs over the potential that sobriety could have offered. She repeatedly decided to crawl back to drug use instead of building a better life for herself and her children.

I could blame my mom for the choices that she made. Her decisions caused pain and heartache for all of her children. I don't make excuses for this. However, in all the things that she did wrong, she did some things right. My mom chose to give us all life, and I love her for this. Life births opportunity, and we are each responsible for the decisions we make with our given opportunities. My mom hadn't yet learned this lesson in her own life, but she would one day embrace what truly mattered. We can't control the circumstances that we are born into, but this does not negate the value of the life that we are given. Everyone deserves a chance to live and learn from experience.

Chapter Two

Shaped by Starvation

Starvation shaped me, pushing me to reject the acceptance that my life would never be better.

I was shaped by starvation. My first memory is the haunting hold of hunger as I ached to be fed. I don't remember much from the earliest years of my childhood, but I remember that. I was always hungry. All of us children were starving, barely kept alive on the scraps of food that we got here and there. The gnawing pain of hunger, my stomach aching to be filled, is a feeling that I will never forget.

At my grandmother's, we had food, and I had formula, which I am sure helped me survive my first year of infancy. My grandmother took over our care, including giving me my first haircut.

My mom was gone for so many months that when she came back to retrieve us, she didn't recognize me.

"Where's my baby at?" she asked my grandmother, her eyes searching the children for the afro puff of hair on the front of my head.

"You're looking at him," replied my grandma, nonplussed. She scooped me up, presenting me to my mother. I stared back at my mom, drooling and sucking on the two fingers that were usually in my mouth.

Embarrassment at not recognizing her child morphed into anger as my mom yelled at my grandmother for cutting my hair. My mom blamed my grandmother for cutting my hair instead of accepting responsibility for being gone for months. Her shame turned into rage as she lashed out.

"How dare you cut my baby's hair without my permission?" she yelled. "I said that you could look after the kids for a while. I didn't say nothin' about letting you cut my baby's hair."

My mom was mad that my hair had been cut, even though it had been her own choices that separated us during that time. She could have been grateful that there was someone who loved us enough to take care of us, but I'm not sure that she considered this. We went from a place of regular feedings to resuming a starvation status far beyond food insecurity. The transition from my grandma back to my mother was turbulent, going from loving care to chaos and neglect. We were yanked from semi-stability with my grandmother back into a place of hunger.

I want to be clear about this—my mother loved us and wanted each of us children. I also want to be clear that neglect or allowing abuse is not love, so I recognize that this is a strange contradiction. She was not trying to place us in a harmful situation, but she did. Her addiction to drugs skewed her decision-making skills.

I don't think that she honestly ever realized how hard things were for us during our childhood. She made a series of bad choices that deeply affected each of us. She loved us, but at the time, drug use made it impossible for her to view life as it truly was and care for us in the way that was needed. When my mom was sober, she cooked and provided for us, much like a typical mom, but when she was not sober, our world was turned upside down.

When we returned from my grandma's, we moved to Guthrie, Oklahoma. Slightly closer to Oklahoma City, my father moved us into a big blue house in town. This house had three bedrooms like our other one, and while probably not much larger, it seemed so to my siblings and me. A larger house did not mean that it was well maintained. We lived in squalor. We crawled and played in urine-soaked diapers and soiled clothing. The house was filthy. There were rats and roaches, and our shared mattresses were saturated with pee, sweat, or other unknown bodily fluids. The smell was horrible, and it was no place for children to thrive.

At this point, my mom's lifestyle consisted of doing drugs, alternated with sporadic periods of work. Sometimes to make a little money, my mom would help my dad. He did janitorial work in buildings around Oklahoma City and in Guthrie. My parents would load all five of us kids into the car and drive us to whatever office building he was working in at the time. Sometimes we would get to come inside and sit and wait in the building, but often we would be stuck in the hot car, sitting alone for hours. I realize that in their minds, locking five children in a car meant we were safe in one place with Kiesha watching us. However, in reality, leaving all five of us a car for hours with only a slightly older child to supervise was extremely unsafe. It didn't matter that I screamed to be fed, or my other siblings were too small to do much more than squabble or cry. Maybe they thought that they were being responsible by dragging us along with them, but they were neglecting us either way. We cried and sobbed, while poor Kiesha did her best to manage us.

Crack was my parents' priority, and in this, we were just afterthoughts. They took care of their own needs and cravings and left us to fend for ourselves with Kiesha doing the best that she could to keep us alive. If my parents were working, they were spending the money that they made on crack as soon as they could get their hands on it.

As an infant, I relied on formula for nourishment. Kiesha knew how to prepare bottles, measure formula, and feed me. Since we had little to no income, our family qualified for food stamps and the supplemental food program for Women, Infants, and Children, better known as WIC. WIC provided nutrition to struggling families like ours, or would have if my mom didn't sell our vouchers for crack. Vouchers supplied formula, milk, cheese, cereal, and all the healthy basics necessary to feed growing children. In reality, my mom might redeem some of our WIC vouchers for food, but often she just sold or traded them for crack. This left my sister desperate to find ways to feed us.

Without formula, there was nothing much that my sister could do to keep me fed. I would cry, sobbing and gnawing on my empty bottles so hard that my tiny gums cut through the rubber nipple as I desperately and instinctually searched for something to fill my stomach.

Sometimes, when cleaning office buildings, my dad would stuff suckers or candy into his pockets to bring home to feed us. Often this was all Kiesha had to use to try to keep us satisfied. Distraught from my lack of food and worried that I was getting no nourishment whatsoever, Kiesha resorted to crushing up candy suckers and feeding the broken pieces to me in an attempt to quench my hunger. She had nothing else to give me, so she made do with what she had, distressed that it was never going to be enough.

Kiesha did her best to try to soothe me, but without food, I was usually inconsolable. Hunger was our constant companion, and there was nothing that Kiesha could do to make that change.

Since my mom sold most of our food vouchers, leaving us with no money or groceries, Kiesha had to get creative. Usually, my mom would use the vouchers to purchase a minimum amount of food while selling or trading the rest for drugs. She would operate similarly with our food stamps, buying us a little food with our monthly allotment, then selling or trading the rest to buy crack.

When my mom did buy us food, it would be scarce and never a complete meal of any sort. We would have peanut butter with no jelly or bread, hotdogs without buns, or stale cereal with no milk. When my mom wasn't high or sleeping, she fed us if we asked, but this was so rare that it couldn't be relied upon with any predictable measure. When she was sober, she provided for us. When she was high, we had to fend for ourselves. My mother's recollection from this time retained the sober moments when things were good, while our memories were imprinted with the trauma of living with addiction and starvation. Our perspectives were shaped by our own experiences.

In those days, food stamps were mailed to us each month, and Kiesha took to watching the mailbox intently. She would take the food stamps from our mailbox, trying to use them before our mom could get her hands on them. She struggled to afford formula to keep the infants from going hungry and tried her best to scour for food for her siblings. If she couldn't buy us food, she would steal what she could, shoplifting little bits here and there to keep us from starvation.

Our utilities were frequently shut off, and Kiesha had to steal water from the neighbors' spigots to try to bathe us or give us something to drink. She would scrounge up candles when the power was turned off, stealing what she could from neighbors or the local store.

If we found food, there was usually a fight for it. We were all so hungry that it was instinctual to devour what we could before our other siblings found it. One day, I discovered a partial stick of margarine and was so hungry that I shoved it in my mouth, gnawing on the cool yellow buttery substance. My siblings noticed my discovery and jumped at the chance to take it for themselves. We were all so hungry that we fought and kicked, scratching and pulling to try to get a bite of it. We battled to get a taste of anything that would squelch our hunger, satisfying us for even the briefest amount of time.

Kiesha was responsible for taking us to school and daycare each day. She struggled with carrying us babies while keeping her raucous group in tow. She trudged along the ten-minute walk to daycare each day, delivering the youngest of us there before she herded the school-age children off toward our local elementary school. My mom insisted that we go to daycare so that the state wouldn't find out what was going on at home and snatch us up into the system.

Any food that we got at school or daycare helped, but did not satisfy our hunger. To us, starvation was tangible as we spent hour after hour with stomachs aching, groaning, and growling, wondering why we couldn't be fed. My first memory is of this feeling, the gnawing of hunger that was never fully satisfied.

Sometimes my dad would bring home sandwiches that he got from work. We never got a full sandwich— just parts or pieces divided among the five of us. We used to think that people who ate bologna and cheese were rich because we didn't know any differently, and that type of food seemed extravagant compared to our meager rationings. That seemed like a sumptuous feast compared to our syrup sandwiches or crushed-up candy. Kiesha would fight and cry with my mom, begging her not to sell the food stamps and pleading with her to feed her babies. It was Kiesha who bore the weight of the starvation that we suffered because she could see our struggle, yet was too young to rescue us.

My dad had another child, a daughter named Erica, that he favored for whatever reason. Erica didn't live with us, but she did visit. She was older than I was by a few years. I don't know if my dad didn't believe that I belonged to him or he simply didn't like me, but while I starved, he would bring Erica to our house with a fresh new Happy Meal or other fast-food treats. She would gleefully eat while the rest of us looked on in envy. We didn't understand why she would get food while all of us went hungry. My dad's preferential treatment of my half-sister angered Kiesha to no end. She was fighting to find anything to feed us, and my dad was giving Erica food in front of us without seeming to care how it made us feel. Whenever Kiesha noticed "Daddy Duncan" wasn't watching, she would take pieces of Erica's Happy Meal to distribute to the other kids.

"Don't you tell your dad," she would threaten the little girl. Erica didn't dare mess with Kiesha. Kiesha nurtured us, but she was also a fierce protector, and if she felt that we were being hurt or slighted, she would do her best to fight for us.

The feeling of hunger that haunted my tiny body in those early years still sticks with me. I can never forget what it felt like to be starving, literally wasting away, while other people watched, not intervening to help. That hunger gave me the drive to do things differently, fighting for what is right and not just standing by while others struggle. Starvation shaped me, pushing me to reject the notion that my life would never be better. It taught me that true hunger means fighting for what is right, working to provide for yourself, and never giving up in the face of desperate circumstances.

Chapter Three

Standing Up to Bullies

If we can't stand on our own, we need to encourage others to stand with us and defend what we know is right.

All stories have bullies. Bullies don't pick on people who are evenly matched in power or strength. No, bullies are weak themselves, so they pick on smaller prey while appearing to be bigger and bolder than they are. In life, there are always bullies. It is unavoidable. In my childhood, there was never a shortage of people who looked to gain power from intimidating or picking on those who were vulnerable.

Although there were always bullies, I learned early on that there are certain people who show true strength by standing up in the face of adversity and saying, "This is enough." These people are not worried about the size of the bully that they are facing, because the strength of their convictions overshadows their fear.

My sister Kiesha was one of these people. If she saw that we were being hurt, neglected, or abused, she fought for us. Undeterred by her own youth, she focused on the problem in front of her and worked to make it better to the best of her ability. Unfortunately, she was put in this position far too often.

When my mom broke up with my dad, we moved again. We left the big blue house and moved into somewhere equally as wretched. We moved so often that the places we lived don't stand out in my mind as individual houses. They blend, intertwining into snapshots of continued poverty, filth, and utter destitution.

The locations changed, and the men that my mom paraded through our lives varied, but there were still some constants: hunger was present, my mom chose crack over us, and there were too many kids and not enough care. We were neglected, starved, and dirty all of the time. Poverty and transient living characterized our existence.

Kiesha still tried her best to provide for us and protect us, but she could only do so much. Her resources were limited to almost nothing. How could she change us if there were no diapers? How could she feed us if there was no food? How could she clean us if there was no water? She stepped up and did what she could.

Since my mom was always having new babies, it seemed that Kiesha had no choice but to miss school to care for them. My mom might call in excuses to cover for the absences, but often she did not. Sometimes daycare was an option, but sometimes it was not. If a child was too young for daycare or was sick and had to stay home, Kiesha ended up caring for them. Eventually, she stopped going to school altogether.

Kiesha fought with my mom all of the time. She hated that my mom wouldn't care for us, feed us, or provide us with the minimum necessities. She resented that my mom would have men over and give them priority over us. She was angry at the injustice of the situation. Although she couldn't always protect us, she didn't sit passively by when she witnessed wrongdoing. She stood up and said something, even at personal cost to her. I recognized the strength that she had in doing this and admired her for it. She fought for others who couldn't fight for themselves, or she rallied others around her to join in her cause.

At eleven years old, Kiesha got pregnant, ramping up the tension between her and my mom. I am sure that it didn't help that my mom was also pregnant at the time. Kiesha thought that she was all grown up at that age. My mom disagreed, but it wasn't as if she willingly shouldered her responsibilities. They fought and fought.

Whenever Kiesha left following a blow-up with my mom, she would disappear for days at a time. She was torn continuously between fighting with my mom and the feelings of responsibility that she had for us. She knew that without her, we would suffer much more than if she was around. This kept her coming back.

Wherever we were living, we lived in complete filth. The house was always dilapidated and disgusting. My mom was still smoking drugs and couldn't afford a safe place for us, so we lived in houses or apartments that were falling to pieces around us. Instead of trying to clean or fix anything up, we just contributed to the disrepair. Roaches crawled over us while we slept, and rats were everywhere. The rats didn't remain hidden away in walls, their scratches haunting our dreams. In one house, the infestation was so bad that I remember seeing rats running past us while we played. Nothing was ever clean. We wore dirty clothes and slept on shared urine-soaked mattresses.

My mom began dating my brother Norman's dad during that time. His name was also Norman—or Big Norman. Kiesha didn't trust him at all. Big Norman would beat us and purposely starve us, taking any food there was for himself. It incensed Kiesha that I seemed to be a particular target for his anger and aggression. My stutter and small size made me an easy mark for his beatings and bullying.

Kiesha did what she could to stand up for us all. When things got terrible, and Big Norman raged, she would gather us all up and take us all to my grandma's house. Eventually, my grandma would send us back, trying her best to get my mother to take responsibility. Whenever we got home, Kiesha would get whooped by my mom for taking us out of the house.

Norman's dad was abusive toward my mom. She was unaware that he was also aggressive toward her children, and we were too young to communicate that.

He was possessive and jealous, not wanting my mom to talk to or interact with other men in any capacity. If he thought that she was looking at another man, he would slap her across the face, leaving her with a black eye.

One day my mom, who was pregnant at the time, was waitressing at a restaurant where she and Big Norman worked. Big Norman was watching her intently, convinced that she was flirting with her boss. She was cooking for her boss when Norman became enraged. My mom attempted to soothe him, explaining that she was just being friendly. He slapped her across the face with an open palm. They were both fired.

He would beat her, and he also terrorized me. As the baby, I was the most vulnerable member of the house, and Norman's dad exploited this. Maybe he was jealous that as a baby, my mom turned her attention toward me and away from him. I don't know, but I do know that this made Kiesha angry.

Kiesha ended up getting kicked out of the house because of her pregnancy, but she and my grandma would check on us when they could. Soon enough, Kiesha's baby was born, and my mother gave birth to my little brother, Norman, Jr. Kiesha would become pregnant twice by the age of thirteen.

Norman's dad continued to beat my mom until she was black and blue, to the point that Kiesha was scared not only for us, but also for my mom. She begged my

Uncle Willie to go look in on us, and upon visiting, he found my mom with both eyes swollen nearly shut from beatings. Uncle Willie took one look at the situation and, enraged, began punching Big Norman. Uncle Willie fought Norman from our house to the city limits, beating him back with each step. He pummeled him until his hands swelled and his knuckles were torn and tender. After that, Norman's dad never returned, sparing us from more abuse. Kiesha had rallied my uncle to protect us, and he didn't just stand idly by. He took action on our behalf, protecting us in the very way that Big Norman used to hurt us.

After this incident, my mom moved us again, this time to Oklahoma City. Kiesha came back to live with us, bringing her own baby.

My mom was also still having babies at seemingly regular intervals. Quinton and Tyrell followed the birth of Norman, and we crowded into whatever house my mom or her man could afford. More babies meant more mouths to feed, and there was still never enough.

By this time, Kiesha figured that she was just as much a grown woman as anybody. She had helped care for six of my mom's kids and her own. She was tired of my mom smoking crack all the time, tired of watching us always going hungry and living in filth, and she didn't like my mom's latest man and how he treated us.

I was still my sister's "Butt-Butt," following her around, stuttering a mile a minute any thought that popped into my head. When she was there, we were all glad to see her. We knew that at least someone would be trying their best to feed us and take care of us, but we were all a bit lost when she was gone.

My mom and Kiesha continued to fight, and she faded in and out of our home. Kiesha would go away for a while, returning to find us in a mess of tears and in terrible condition. She would stay as long as she could manage, leaving again when she fought with my mom. She felt that we needed her, but warring with my mom was too difficult.

Over and over, Kiesha fought for us, intervening to protect us or take care of us, rallying others on our behalf. She needed others to do the same for her: supporting her, advocating for her, and fighting for her, but no one did. We were too young to help her, and she was pushed to grow up before she was ready.

It wasn't long before Kiesha was pregnant again and back with us for a more extended period. Quinton's dad was living with us and would keep food from us. We were already always hungry, but he would withhold food from us to punish us for merely existing. He devised a system where only a few of us would be fed at each meal. He would lock us in various rooms, and only the room with the kids he chose would get to eat.

He would put his kids in my mom's room and allow them to eat while the rest would go hungry. More often than not, he only chose to feed his kids while the rest of us went without, our bodies and brains sluggish from malnutrition. When Kiesha found out, she hit the roof, hollering and screaming and fighting with him and my mom. My mom had her arrested. Kiesha was nine months pregnant at the time, but she was taken to jail. Eventually Kiesha's life got too complicated, and she had to give her own two children to the Department of Human Services (DHS).

I wish that I could say that I dreamed of a life where everything was different, but at that time, I didn't know that life could be any different. The chaos, starvation, violence, abuse, and neglect were all usual to me. I just wanted to fill my aching stomach and survive the challenges that each day presented.

I hadn't yet learned to stand up and fight for myself, but I had seen Kiesha do that consistently for us. This left a strong impression in my mind. It taught me that if we see injustice, we need to address it and stand up for what is right. If we encounter bullies, we need to hold them accountable and protect the vulnerable. We may not feel strong or prepared, but that doesn't mean that we should not fight for what is right. If we can't stand on our own, we need to encourage others to stand with us and defend what we know is right.

Chapter Four

Yo-Yo Kids

We were like human yo-yos being bounced back and forth between foster care and the erratic care of our mom.

y television debut wasn't viral or career-launching. It captured a sad, desperate situation. A family struggling caught was on film. My grandmother watched us on TV as the news showed my family in chaos as we tumbled from a house on fire, babies screaming, their diapers sagging and soaked from not being changed. One of the derelict houses that we were staying in had caught on fire, and it was all over the local news.

We had been left unattended, and a fire broke out. My mother was down the street, smoking crack, and one of my brothers was playing around with things that he shouldn't have been. He started a fire that rapidly spread throughout the house. The general disrepair of the house probably helped to fuel the fire, and before long, we were dragged out of it, scared, screaming, and coughing as smoke filled our little lungs.

By this time, we had previously been taken from my mother and put in foster care. I don't remember the first time it happened, but I remember it happening this time. Neglect and poor care were evident as the police gathered up the children in my family and loaded us in police cars to transport us to the shelter. We were dirty, our tear-streaked faces smudged. I sat silently numb, observing while my other siblings cried out in anguish. Some of them kicked and fought, struggling and screaming, not understanding why they would be taken from our mother.

I sat staring out the window of the police cruiser, silently internalizing my pain. The truth is that I am not sure I knew what to think. My mom was not perfect by any standard, but she was all that I really knew, and I instinctually loved her. It was terrifying to be taken from the familiar and placed into a new and equally unpredictable situation. There was trauma in staying with my mom and the conditions in which we were living. There was also trauma in being forced into a shelter and pushed into the homes of strangers, not knowing what life would be like from one minute to another.

My siblings and I were used to chaos, ever-changing circumstances that only seemed to worsen. Even though we lived in horrific conditions at home, that was all we knew. There was a strange sort of twisted comfort in that. When removed from our mother's care, it stripped us of the security of our normal, no matter how neglectful that normal was. We would cry and beg to stay with our mom, our grandma, or Kiesha.

I was probably about four when I first entered the foster care system. I was so young that it is hard to pin down a precise age, but once I was in the system, it became like a revolving door of stays: in and out, in and out. My sister, Kiesha, and my brother, Ricky, ran away, and child services couldn't track them down. This kept them out of the foster care system. The social workers were too overwhelmed to track down two teens that didn't want to go into the system.

The rest of us would be in care for a few months while my mom worked on reunification, then back with her until the authorities found us neglected again, abandoned in favor of crack. When my mother was on drugs, she wasn't mentally stable enough to care for her children. That is the bottom line. My mom couldn't do drugs and be a fit mother at the same time. She had to get clean to take care of us in any adequate way. She wanted us but wanted drugs more. If she stayed clean even for a short time, she would always relapse. When this inevitably happened, the social workers and court system would gather us all up and back into foster care we would go.

My grandma tried to get permission to care for us to keep us out of foster care. She had a four-bedroom home and was willing to take us in, even though it would have been a challenge. She offered to keep us but was denied. She was told initially by the social worker that she already was watching too many kids and didn't have enough room for us. That may have been true, but I also know that in those days, there was a concern about giving children to a relative that had a close relationship with the parent. They were worried that this would provide the parent access without permission, and the parent might continue to harm the children. I am sure that my grandma wouldn't have put up with any nonsense from my mother, but the state social workers had no way of knowing that.

We were like human yo-yos being bounced back and forth between foster care and the erratic care of our mom. We couldn't settle anywhere because we never knew when we would be snatched out of any little bit of comfort that we found. We were always on edge, our little bodies on hyper-alert, looking for danger in all situations. Some of us withdrew, and some acted out, unbridled anger taking over. We all processed the trauma of the situation in our own ways. We were sad, hurting, and uncertain about what each day was going to bring, rebounding back and forth between places of fear and uncertainty.

Chapter Five

Fostered by the System

*I knew instinctively that there was
an opportunity for me to grow in whatever
situation that I faced.*

Unpredictability fosters adaptability. When you are continually placed into new situations, you can respond by crumbling, or with flexibility, relying on the knowledge that no matter how difficult things seem, they eventually will improve. You can experience internal growth from your circumstance's unpredictability, or you can fixate on anger and hurt, being dragged under by these overwhelming emotions. Adaptability in the face of unpredictable outcomes is a skill. For me, this skill was refined in the foster care system.

Every time we entered into foster care, the process was virtually the same. The social workers or police would come and pick us up. There would be screaming, crying, and kids running in all directions. Some of us kids were stoic, while others were heart-wrenching in their histrionics. My usually cheerful chatter became almost non-existent as I sat mouth open, watching the conflict unfold before me, resigned that it was nothing that I had even the slightest bit of control over.

Once we loaded into the various police cars, authorities drove us to the children's shelter. The shelter that we were placed in had an official name, but to us, it was just the DHS Children's Center. Some states have Child Protective Services (CPS), but in our state, the foster care oversight fell to the Department of Human Services (DHS). A big, barren-looking brick building housed the children's shelter, and it was where all the children who were removed from their parents temporarily went until they could be placed in longer-term foster care home situations. The brightly painted interior didn't dampen the feelings of uncertainty and fear that each visit to this emergency shelter brought.

When we were taken from our mother, there was no other place to go. The process was always the same. DHS snatched us from our home, as everyone screamed and cried. They would then drive us down to the shelter because they didn't have another place to put children immediately. No one ever knew if we would be spending days in the shelter, or weeks. It was always chaotic and confusing.

While we were in the shelter, they would try to place us with an available family. DHS did their best to attempt to keep siblings together. However, with a family as large as mine, no one was equipped to house us all. One child is hard to place; two siblings are even more difficult. Sibling groups of three or more rarely get placed together, but a family the size of mine being housed together was a virtual impossibility. Aside from hunger and neglect, my siblings were the only other constant in my early childhood, so it was hard to be separated from them.

I have never been to prison, but I imagine the shelter process is similar to the check-in at a prison. It was always the same. The workers checked us in, making sure that they had all of our correct information. They told us to give them all of our belongings, and they promised to give them back when we left. The truth was that we would most likely never see those belongings again. They stuffed the items in black plastic bags that might or might not have been labeled correctly. I lost so many cherished items to this process when I never had much to begin with. The loss of some of those things still makes me mad. We would come into the shelter with nothing but the few things that we had a connection with or that had value to us. It was devastating to us children to be told that these were lost and we would not be getting them back as we left. It still bothers me that there were so many small, meaningful items that were never returned to me or other kids like me who went through the same process.

Not only did they take our things, but they took our clothes as well. We were never allowed to wear our own clothes. They gave us a uniform of blue jeans and a white T-shirt to wear while we were there. Girls and boys were housed on entirely separate sides of the building. The girls were on one side and the boys were on the other, and they didn't mix. That meant that my brothers and I were always separated from my sister, Lanana. Each child was assigned a room. Sometimes I shared a room with a sibling, but I was often assigned to a room with a child I had never met before.

Each day in the shelter functioned in a strictly organized routine. I think that the routine was meant to provide some semblance of stability in our otherwise tumultuous lives. They endeavored to design some predictability into our otherwise unpredictable childhoods. However, the routine of the shelter did nothing to combat the chaos that we each felt battling inside.

Each day I would wake up and join a line at the clothes closet. A worker would be standing there. He or she would size me up, measuring by dangling a white T-shirt in front of me, eyeballing it to see if it would make a good fit. The worker would hand me my shirt, doing the same thing with jeans, guesstimating the approximate size. Once I had my clothes and hygiene box, I would be sent to wait with the other kids for my shower turn. I would scrub myself clean, get dressed, and file back into line for the next activity.

After that, I would eat breakfast in the cafeteria, go outside for outdoor recess, and play on the jungle gym or swing sets. The play area was surrounded by high brick walls that kept the kids from trying to run away. I think that the workers tried their best to make it a fun place, but overall it was just a sad environment, full of hurting kids.

If the weather was bad, we would be occupied with inside games or crafts, getting sticky with whatever glue, paint, or glittery mess we were instructed to create. In this way, it wasn't that much different than a daycare. I would play with the other kids, but I didn't ever make any real friends. It was too transient, with kids coming in and then leaving for homes, to count on making any sort of permanent bonds.

After playtime or fun indoor activities, we would return to the cafeteria for lunch, followed by TV time. After we watched TV for a while, we would have dinner followed by a movie. They gave us a snack and then sent us off to our rooms for bed.

Once we were in our rooms for the night, we were locked in. They would lock the doors from the outside, the click-click of the lock ensuring that we couldn't leave our rooms until morning wakeup. I dreaded going there. The daily routine didn't ease the uncertainty of not knowing where I would be going or how long I would be separated from my family.

The routine of the shelter may have been predictable, but the children were not. Most of the kids were nice, but some children in the shelter were particularly challenging. My small stature and stutter made me an easy target for bullies. There was one particularly vicious boy. A much larger child would knock me around, destroy my stuff, and bully me relentlessly. One day, out of nowhere, he punched me hard in the throat. I thought I was about to die as I coughed and sputtered, trying to draw in oxygen. My throat hurt for a week after that, feeling as if I swallowed a bucket full of nails.

I know that most kids in the shelter were hurting emotionally, and lashing out was a typical result of trying to process the overwhelming emotions. Still, that boy was particularly brutal in his bullying, and I was his favorite target.

The routine of the shelter was helpful, but it only gave the illusion of organization and some sort of semblance of control. In reality, it was filled with children who had absolutely no power in their lives and whose only certainty was uncertainty and trauma. The bully who often beat me projected his trauma and pain onto others, harming them and himself in the process. Other children withdrew, letting no one in, isolating themselves from connection. I can't really say how I responded at the time. I was a mass of mixed-up emotions, and I probably did not handle it correctly. Yet, I was also resilient. I knew instinctively that there was an opportunity for me to grow in whatever situation that

I faced. I could crumble, or I could stand firm. I could be a victim, or I could adapt and thrive. Even as a child, I had to make a choice. I could fall deep into a well of victimhood and despair, or I could focus on what I had control over. This wasn't much, but it was something. I could control my outlook and my response to the situation. I chose to adapt to life changes with positivity and as much joy and laughter as I could manage.

Foster care is a tough and desolate place, but there are bright spots. A foster family that provides a safe and loving home for a child can illuminate a child's path to a solid future. Thankfully, God provided me such a family when I was assigned to stay with the Solomons.

The heartbreaking truth about foster care is that most people don't want anything to do with it. People love rallying around causes for children, but they are suspiciously absent when asked to take children into their homes. There are far more foster children then there are homes to place them in, and this is a continual problem.

It strikes me as strange that people seem to care about abused and neglected pets more than hurting and abandoned children. Pet owners are encouraged to adopt pets from shelters instead of planned puppies so that no pet is left alone, yet for children, the opposite is true. A foster child is usually seen as someone who is damaged beyond repair, contributing nothing positive to a new potential family. While shelter dogs are trendy, housing foster children is viewed as potentially dangerous and disruptive. This observation is in no way a discouragement of dog adoption or a comparison of dogs to children. It is merely something that I have noticed and which our attention should be drawn. Children deserve to be loved and cared for without their trauma being held against them. They need a chance, an opportunity to be nurtured and grow.

Thankfully, I was given that chance. The first foster home that I remember being placed in was the Solomons, and they were extraordinary. A married couple in their sixties, they raised their children and then ended up adopting and taking care of some of their grandchildren. They had a real heart for children, and they had a great home for a scared little boy to be placed.

Mrs. Solomon welcomed me into her house with a warm smile and a kind greeting. "You can call me Maw-Maw," she said, the smell of good southern cooking wafting toward me.

Maw-Maw toured me around the house and introduced me to her two grandchildren. She showed me where I would be sleeping and where I would store my belongings. A few minutes later, the backdoor opened, and Mr. Solomon came in.

"Hi there," he introduced himself, brushing dirt off his sleeve. "You can call me Pap-Paw."

The Solomons lived on an active farm in central Oklahoma. They were hard workers who loved children. Many people foster as a way to bless kids, which is commendable, but the Solomons also saw that the reverse is true. They knew that foster children could enrich their lives, as well. An excellent foster family can be wonderful for a child, but to foster a child is also a privilege and blessing to the family that takes him in.

The Solomons didn't need more children, but they saw the value in something that few people seem to understand. They had a family that they could share with a child who needed a family. They had a home that could welcome a homeless child. The Solomons had a love that they could give to a child who didn't know love. Maw-Maw and Paw-Paw believed in changing the world one child at a time.

Their family gave me the stability that I so desperately needed. Life on the farm was hard work, but it was fun. I would tag along behind Paw-Paw as he taught me how to work on the farm.

"Clarence, come help me out in the yard," he bellowed, the rich timbre of his voice carrying to Maw-Maw while she worked in the kitchen.

"It is Terrence," she hollered back at him with a laugh. "John, his name is not Clarence. It is Terrence."

Paw-Paw knew that my name was Terrence, but the name Clarence stayed in his mind for some reason. It wasn't out of lack of care or out of malicious intent. He just could never get it right. It didn't bother me, though. If he called, I came running just as fast as my tiny legs could carry me, excited to follow him around the farm.

Paw-Paw was a hard worker himself and didn't allow slacking in others. However, he didn't just boss other people around. He worked shoulder to shoulder with them to accomplish the tasks for that day. He had grown up picking cotton and embraced hard work. Every day we tended the cows, cared for the horses, and kept the barn clean. I had daily chores that I learned to keep up with and helped in the field.

In the evenings, Maw-Maw would gather us all around for a large dinner of gumbo, jambalaya, or whatever delicious meal she had prepared. Originally from Louisiana, Maw-Maw knew everything there was about how to make a true southern-style mouth-watering meal. Her cooking was like heaven on earth for a child who was used to a belly full of emptiness.

Maw-Maw and Paw-Paw had two grandchildren that they were raising. Initially, my sister Lanana and I were both supposed to be placed on the farm with them, but for whatever reason, my sister asked to go to a different family. Throughout the time that I was there, Maw-Maw and Paw-Paw welcomed in whatever children they could. I was rarely ever the only foster child in their care as they opened their doors to children with challenges that some other families might shy away from. In this, they lived love.

The Solomons gave my life a comfortable routine and predictability that it had otherwise lacked. I knew that each day there would be chores to be completed, that I would never go hungry, and that all my needs would be met. They gave me a safe place to stay, toys to play with, new clothes, and plenty of food. They offered the needed love and stability that I had been missing. There was security in the normality of it all.

It was on their farm that I began the transition from simply surviving life to learning how to thrive. The Solomons treated me just like any other member of their family. I still had visitations with my mom from time to time and I missed her, but I was at peace within the Solomons' household. They made sure that I had had everything that I needed from a practical standpoint while nourishing me emotionally through the time and energy that they invested in me.

The Solomons taught me how to ride a bike for the first time, earning a scar across my stomach for my efforts when I went flying into a tree. They patiently listened to me stutter out broken sentences without growing frustrated, but they also arranged for me to have speech therapy lessons. Paw-Paw let me follow him on the farm, teaching me how to mow the yard and taking me with him in his big pickup truck that he started with an old screwdriver. I tagged along when he went to help neighbors with downed trees or other tasks. His time was precious, yet he shared it with me.

Every night we prayed together, and I learned how to thank God and ask Him for what I needed. Every Sunday, we dressed in our best and went to church. Maw-Maw and Paw-Paw took me to church each week, and I was enthralled by the biblical stories of how God perfectly used even the most imperfect people. I knew that I would never be perfect, but I prayed that God would use me, too. I learned to memorize the books of the Bible, and my relationship with God grew little by little.

I didn't just learn about God in church; I learned about His love through the Solomons' faithfulness. The Bible says, "God is love," and they tried to model this in their own lives. They were not perfect, but they may have been the best example that I had up to that time of a 1 Corinthians 13 kind of love.

I began kindergarten while I lived with Maw-Maw and Paw-Paw. They got me registered and made sure that I had everything that I needed for my first day of school. They helped me to learn to read and were very proud of me when I came home with excellent report cards. They would reward my good grades with a new Sunday church outfit or Sunday shoes. I felt special as I dressed my best to go to church each week, but I felt even more special that Maw-Maw and Paw-Paw were proud of me.

Maw-Maw and Paw-Paw helped me learn how to be a child, taking on the burden of simple things that troubled me considerably, such as where my next meal would come from. They instilled in me a sense of pride in a job well done by having high expectations for my performance of the expected chores. They taught me early skills like tying my shoes and practicing kindness for others. They helped me to learn how to tease and laugh. Even something as basic as a haircut could turn into a lesson of love.

Whenever I returned from a visit to the barber, Paw-Paw would exclaim, "Who is that? Who is that? Who is this little man up in my house?"

He would then call to Maw-Maw, "Where's Clarence? This little man just walked here saying he's Clarence. Where's my little boy, Clarence?"

She would shake her head, placing her soft brown hand gently on my head and oblige him in his joking, "John, this here is your boy, Terrence. Doesn't his haircut look so handsome?"

I would smile and laugh. "Paw-Paw, it's me, Terrence. I'm right here."

I lived with them for several years, and I know that they would have adopted me if the courts allowed it. My mom had parental rights and was still trying to earn us back. My mom was heartbroken to have lost her kids, but she was struggling to remain sober. She went to rehab and underwent drug testing, trying to get us back. We would see her at visitations, and we knew that she wanted us. At first, we did think that we would be back with her before long, but over time, we realized that this just wasn't going to happen.

I knew that my mom must have loved me because she always wanted me back, but she wasn't yet living the love that I learned about in church. I was conflicted between missing my mom and enjoying my contentment within the Solomon family.

Maw-Maw was from Louisiana, and Paw-Paw was from Mississippi. They planned to move back south eventually. After living with the Solomons for a few years, I learned that my mom was going to get me back. While I prepared to leave the Solomons' loving house, they were preparing to move as well.

Maw-Maw's mother was sick, and she needed someone to care for her, so the Solomons decided that they would move back to Louisiana. If I had been given a choice, I would have moved with them. I wanted to stay with Maw-Maw and Paw-Paw forever. However, as a foster child, my mother had rights, and until these rights were terminated, I couldn't move out of the state.

After several years with Maw-Maw and Paw-Paw, I had collected a good amount of possessions for a school-aged child. The Solomons had given me clothes, toys, books, a bike—really anything that I could have ever needed. They helped me carefully pack my belongings to take everything with me back to my mom's house.

I didn't cry when my mom came. She was my mom, so I knew that I belonged with her somehow, but I felt I belonged with the Solomons, too.

"Aww... baby, don't you worry," soothed Mrs. Solomon, as she helped me get ready. "We'll see you again."

In his gruff yet kind way, Mr. Solomon assured, "Clarence, we'll stay in touch. We'll see you again. That's my boy, Clarence. You take good care of him," he instructed my mother.

My mother told me that we would not be taking my stuff from the Solomons. "Your siblings will be jealous. They don't have all that stuff. You leave it here."

Maw-Maw was incensed. She didn't see any point in that. She couldn't understand why I would have to leave behind the stuff that belonged to me. They bought it for me. They had given it to me. I deserved good things. Why should I have to leave my belongings and bike behind?

I left the Solomons' house with nothing, and at my mom's house, she had almost nothing for me there. It didn't make any sense to me. Once again, I was a yo-yo kid, bounced out of the safety and security with the Solomons in exchange for upheaval.

Chapter Seven

Conflicting Feelings

This is not my home,
and you are not my mama.

*T*his is not my home, and you are not my mama.
I silently seethed as Mrs. Scarborough glared
down at me, her tall frame accentuating her
severe features. Hateful to her core, she had heard me
crack my knuckles and intended to punish me for my
misstep.

She whipped me and my brother Norman at the
slightest provocation, but often she implemented a slow-
er, more extended form of torture. The beatings were
cruel, but at least they didn't go on endlessly. Punished
for the accidental sound of my knuckle popping, I was
to spend hours standing in a corner, with my knees
slightly bent and my arms extended.

My arms ached and burned after only a few minutes, the muscles in my legs began to shudder, trembling in exhaustion. Searing pain pulsed throughout
my body, but I knew that Mrs. Scarborough would in-
flict much worse torment if I left my position. My tiny
frame quivered and shook as my time in this cramped
posture crawled slowly onward. Mrs. Scarborough was
as mean as Satan with the temperament to match. She

was a harsh disciplinarian, punishing us for any flaw, imperfection, or sign that we were enjoying life as typical kids are supposed to. There were strict rules about everything: we were not welcome in the living room, no television, no games, and no playing allowed. She held us to obsessive standards regarding our appearance and ironed clothing. If even the minutest belt loops weren't tended to with the iron, she would beat us.

For a woman like this to be fostering children seemed to make no sense. She clearly hated us. I didn't understand why the state would take us away from my mama and send us to live with this witch. At home, we may have been starving and neglected while my mom left us to chase after her addictions, but we were together, and sometimes we had Kiesha to care for us.

My mom had earned each of us children back from our respective foster homes. After all, the goal of foster care is reunification—trying to educate and help parents to become better so that they can be there for their children. My mom wanted us back, and she tried to follow the court's instructions. She went to rehab, attended visitations, and spoke to our social workers. She was off drugs, had a job, and secured a place for all of us to stay, begging the judge to give us back. The thing that she could never do for long, however, was remain off drugs.

When I first got to my mom's place after the Solomons, she was clean. There was food—not a lot, but at least there was some. My mom was working to show the court that she had the means to provide for us. This did not last long.

Maw-Maw had tucked a twenty-dollar bill in my hand when I left the Solomons' house and told me to save it for something special. When my mom saw it, she took it, claiming she needed to buy bleach. I never saw any part of it again. Within a few weeks of picking me up from the Solomons, my siblings and I were taken back into the system. My mom was on the path to a better way of life, but she chose drugs over us again.

We found ourselves back at the DHS Children's Center, our social workers buzzing around to try to find new placements for the six of us that they had rounded up.

"Hey, y'all. It's the Williams kids," teased one of the workers. "I knew that you all would be back again soon."

Though said in jest, this remark cut deeply. If the workers didn't have faith in my mom's ability to keep us, our hope must be false. It was disheartening.

I had been with the Solomons steadily for a few years, but my siblings had all had varying stays with different foster families, spending time in and out of the children's shelter. Once again, we were thrust into the uncertainty and instability of not knowing where we would go next.

When I went back to the shelter, Mr. Solomon heard about it. While Maw-Maw was in Louisiana looking after her mother, he was in Mississippi at the time visiting family. As soon as Paw-Paw heard that I was in the shelter, he got in his car and drove from Mississippi to Oklahoma to try to bring "his boy, Clarence, back."

When he got to Oklahoma, Paw-Paw tried his best to get me back, but the social workers remained firm. "No, you can't take Terrence back with you. You live out of state now. He needs to stay in Oklahoma. That is not allowed."

At the time, I didn't know that any of this was occurring. Once again, if I had been given a choice, I would have gone with Paw-Paw in a heartbeat. I missed Maw-Maw and Paw-Paw terribly. I missed their love, their wisdom, their time, and their farm. I missed being cared for and truly loved. If I couldn't have a healthy and whole version of my mom, then I wanted the Solomons to be my family.

I understand the decision to keep me in Oklahoma. My mom was still trying to get us back. She wasn't necessarily working as hard as she could, but that was part of the problem of her addiction to drugs. Her decision-making skills were affected, and she wasn't in a good position mentally to make wise choices, especially regarding emotional decisions such as what was best for her children. My mom believed that her children were safest when they were with her. Children should be with their parents, but when the parents are not able to take care of their children or are harming them, then this is where foster care becomes essential. At the time, I don't think that my mom could see how much her behavior was hurting us. She just wanted us back, or in place of that, wanted us near our siblings if possible. For these reasons, allowing me to go with the Solomons would have never been a possibility that she would have entertained.

Did I want to go with the Solomons? Yes. Did I also want to be with my mom? Yes. Both answers were true. I think that a lot of foster kids experience these conflicting emotions, but it is okay for them to feel both ways. It is okay for them to love their parents and want to be with them, even if they are dysfunctional. It is okay for them to want to stay with and enjoy a foster family that is kind to them. It doesn't have to be one or the other. They can have both feelings and not feel guilty.

My desire to be with the Solomons wasn't about how much I loved my mom. I loved my mom as much as any young boy does, but there was a negative difference in how she cared for us. I don't just mean the level of poverty. Certainly, I had more things at the Solomons. When I went back to live with my mom, I was allowed to bring nothing, and my things were replaced with nothing. We lived in a small house, crowded with kids who lacked basic things that I had become accustomed to having. My mom was there, but gone was the stabilizing force of regular meals, nightly prayers, weekly Sunday church services, consistent chores, wise counsel, and intentional time invested in me.

The Solomons were devastated when I was placed back into the system. They had moved away with the hopes that my mom would finally make things right and keep us safe for good. They were shocked when only a few weeks had gone by, and we were taken right back.

Instead of being placed in another loving home, my younger brother Norman and I were placed with Mrs. Scarborough and her tirades of abuse. The upside of foster care is amazing families like the Solomons, who open their homes out of love to help children. Mrs. Scarborough wasn't one of these great families. She was pure evil.

Chapter Eight

Speaking Out

I have grown to realize that speaking out about what is wrong is a powerful thing.

The smell of buttery popcorn filled my nostrils as I walked excitedly around the gleaming maple floors of the basketball court, finding my seat up in the bleachers. The Harlem Globetrotters gathered on the court to humiliate the opposing team, performing basketball tricks combined with humor, a routine that left my brother and me on the edge of our seats. We watched the players in awe. Dressed in their star-spangled red, white, and blue uniforms, the players entertained, seeming to dance across the court with the fluidity of their sophisticated moves and intricate trick shots.

Mean Mrs. Scarborough had somehow secured tickets for my brother and me to attend this glorious event. Was it a gesture of kindness on her part? Not a chance. Even kidnappers take kids to fun events sometimes. She did nothing without motive or manipulation.

"It is so nice how you have taken those poor kids in," people would say to her. They had no idea that she was beating us black and blue with her belt at the slightest provocation. If I cracked even one knuckle, she would beat me. If the waistband of my jeans wasn't ironed as precisely as she demanded, the belt came out. If my brother and I tried to play, she beat us both, flying into a rage.

She was the complete opposite of the Solomons and should have never been allowed to foster children. Eventually, I was able to report these whoopings to my social worker, and we were removed from Mrs. Scarborough's home. Foster children are not supposed to receive any corporal type of discipline, and Mrs. Scarborough was using far worse than that.

One devastating part of foster care is the abuse that can occur. Often children are taken out of a traumatic situation and placed into an equally traumatizing environment. I was able to report the violation of Mrs. Scarborough and was believed, resulting in our removal from that home. This is not always the case. Often the victims of abuse report it, and it is not believed. Foster kids suffer in silence as they are molested or abused. When they are brave enough to try to voice the terror of the situation, they are ignored in favor of the adults who are hiding their evil actions. These children need a voice and for that voice to be heard.

I was brave enough to report what was happening with Mrs. Scarborough, but I was still finding my own voice. I had seen Kiesha stand up to bullies, but I wasn't always strong enough to defend or stand up for myself. I was sexually molested in foster care multiple times, usually by other kids, and shame kept me silent. I internalized the hurt, confusion, and pain that I felt, and I found ways to blame myself instead of laying the responsibility at the abusers' feet.

To those who are struggling with these feelings as I did, let me be clear about this. Abuse is never your fault. Let me say it again a little bit louder: ABUSE IS NEVER YOUR FAULT! You should never bear the burden of someone else's destructive behavior.

I have grown to realize that speaking out about what is wrong is a powerful thing. When we hold shame inside, it only hurts us and doesn't hold the perpetrator accountable. Sometimes the shame of the abuse makes us feel as if we would be rejected if anyone knows our secret. Abusers thrive when secrets are kept.

Sharing our story has power. Speaking out about abuse can stop it. Sharing the things that we feel shame about allows us to realize that others have gone through similar situations and we are not alone. Discussing the hard stuff may open the door to help to lift another person's burden. If sharing my story can help another person find hope and healing, then it is well worth it.

I wasn't always able to speak up for myself, but I am thankful that I learned from the people who did.

It helped me to heal and gave me a voice. It taught me that we need to stand up to evil, corruption, and abuse, using the power of our words to influence and defeat injustice.

Chapter Nine

Put Your Money Where Your Motor Mouth Is

It is one thing to talk and never be heard and another thing entirely to make an impact with your words.

I was still learning to speak up for myself, but let me tell you, my stutter never held me back from talking. It took me so long to get the words out that you might think that would have stopped me from speaking, but I had a lot to say. My stuttered statements spilled out in a torrent of endless chatter.

I talked nonstop. The stuttering did not deter me from expressing myself. It may have slowed my speech down, but it did not stop me from talking. I was always talking, to the point that I gained the dubious reputation of being a chatterbox in school.

I had started second grade at the Solomons, but after a stint with my mom and Mrs. Scarborough, I had to repeat the second grade. Due to this, I was usually both the smallest and the oldest child in the class. I was also typically the most talkative. It was rare that I didn't have something to say.

My third-grade teacher nicknamed me Motor Mouth because my mouth would be going a mile a minute as I talked about anything and everything that crossed my mind. She couldn't get me to shut up.

When I stuttered, the kids would laugh and call me Stuttering Stanley, which I didn't understand. I definitely stuttered, but couldn't figure out who this Stanley kid was. Their teasing didn't stop me from talking. If anything, it probably gave me more to talk about. They would tease me, and then I would laugh, jawing about why I was laughing at them.

It was around this time that I gained a best friend. His name was "John-Boy, Jr." Back in those days, my elementary school, Parker Elementary, still believed in corporal punishment, and they would whoop us. Each classroom teacher had a small wooden paddle, nicknamed John-Boy, Jr., that they would swat us with if we got out of line. These days, kids don't know what a paddle is, but back then, my elementary school would give us a whooping if we misbehaved. They would swat at our backside for any infraction. John-Boy, Jr., and I spend a lot of time bonding due to my motor mouth.

John-Boy was much larger than John-Boy, Jr., so he resided in the principal's office. If we were really bad, then we got whooped by the big ole John-Boy paddle.

Teachers would call the office: "Sir, we have a child that needs to spend some time with John-Boy. Yes, we tried John-Boy, Jr., but this kid won't stop talking."

The big John-Boy would be brought out only if a student was in a lot of trouble, but to be honest, I met

John-Boy a couple of times, and I didn't like him one bit. John-Boy would tear me up.

Talking a lot was a minor offense, which is how John-Boy, Jr., and I became best friends. The teachers couldn't shut me up, so they tried to curb my talking by using John-Boy, Jr., to remind me to stay quiet. I had a lot to say, so John-Boy, Jr., and I spent way too much time together.

John-Boy wasn't used on chatterboxes, but he was used when we talked back to a teacher. It was rare that I talked back to a teacher, but if I did, then I spent some time with John-Boy and the principal. John-Boy and I were not friends. I tried to avoid him at all costs.

Despite my closeness with the paddle known as John-Boy, Jr., I was quite a good student. I talked a lot and clowned around, but I also always managed to get my schoolwork done and maintain good grades. I loved learning, so this made school easy for me. I worked hard at school, which helped to make up for the fact that I talked so much. My teachers couldn't get too frustrated with me as long as I got my work done and made good grades.

As I grew older, my talking didn't diminish. After years of speech therapy, my stutter had gotten less noticeable, which only increased my talking. I started gaining a reputation for being funny, and this encouraged me. In class, I would hold court, making the other students laugh as I joked about one thing or another.

If John-Boy and John-Boy, Jr., couldn't beat the talking out of me, I don't know that anything could. I think that my talkative nature and the ability to laugh at life's daily challenges were good things, but my teachers didn't always see it that way.

When I was in high school, my math teacher, Mr. M., used to get very frustrated with my talking.

"Terrence, how hard is it to be quiet? How hard is it to keep your mouth shut for one class period?" He would say in aggravation. "Just be quiet!"

I would try, but evidently I didn't try hard enough.

"Terrence, let's talk outside," instructed Mr. M. I followed him outside, scared that I was about to be suspended.

"Tonight is the awards banquet," he informed me. "I was going to present these three awards to you," he said, fanning them out in front of me. Each award was different. One was for the most improvement with my grades, one was for being a good Samaritan and helping other students in the class, and I think that the final one was for academic achievement. I didn't get to glance at them for long before he snatched them away.

He tore each of the awards up in front of me and said, "I was going to give you these awards, but you can't even shut up. Get back to class and be quiet."

"Wow," I said. "Well, damn."

He was right, I was causing disruption in class, but pulling a Pelosi and ripping those papers up didn't inspire me to keep quiet.

The talking probably covered some inner turmoil, but it also gave me a voice to express myself. I had been in and out of a variety of foster homes after my stay at Mrs. Scarborough's house. Some were bad, some were good, but most of them I didn't have a strong feeling about either way.

In my childhood, I was shuffled around so much from foster home to foster home that I often felt that my voice didn't matter. When I was in class or at school and could talk with a captive audience, I knew that my voice mattered and that there were people who were willing to listen to me. This was important. It is one thing to talk and never be heard and another thing entirely to make an impact with your words. I wanted my words to matter.

Chapter Ten

Snapping Back

*Just because a child had both a mother
and a father, this did not mean that he was
in any way better than I was.*

"You are just a stupid crack-baby," yelled one of my classmates. "I know why you don't have a mama or a daddy. They didn't want you because you were nothing but a crack-baby."

"Crack-baby! Crack-baby!" The other kids taunted.

Earlier in my life, these insults would have broken me and caused me to cry or withdraw, but as I got older, I got better at standing up to the bullies and snapping back.

The kids at school knew that my parents weren't around and would tease me for it. "You ain't got no mama because nobody wanted a crack-baby."

This was hurtful, but often the worst insults came from inside foster homes from my foster siblings.

"You can't have my mama just because yours didn't want you! We don't want you either, you stupid crack baby." The words of a jealous foster sibling would slice me deeply.

I think that their words hurt so badly because there was some truth in them. I was most likely a crack-baby, my mom couldn't take care of us, and I didn't have a daddy that I could even remember.

I was teased so often that eventually I stopped feeling the pain of these words. As I stopped feeling the stab of hurt associated with each of these insults, I began to examine them more rationally. Yes, it was true that I didn't have a daddy or mommy around, but that wasn't my fault. I couldn't own their problems. They had an issue with drugs. This was their problem, not mine. If I had been a crack baby, there wasn't anything that I could do about it. I wasn't in foster care because of something that I had done wrong. I was in foster care because of other people's actions. Realizing this empowered me.

I hope that if you are reading this and you have been in foster care or are in foster care, it will empower you as well. Although we are each responsible for our actions, we are not responsible for the actions of others. It wasn't my fault that my parents hadn't taken care of me the way that they should have, so I didn't need to bear the emotional burden. I had to learn to recognize that being a foster child was not something that I caused by doing anything wrong. It was not my fault. If you are in foster care, it is not your fault!

Just as I learned to recognize that it wasn't my fault that I was in the foster care system, I also learned a few other things. Being in foster family after foster family showed me that even though my family had problems, there is no perfect family out there. It simply doesn't exist. Just because a child had both a mother and a father, this did not mean that he was in any way better than I was.

I soon realized that all the statistics that emphasize the negative aspects about the foster care experience, and the numbers that show us why foster kids shouldn't be successful, do not take into account some specific things. They add up all the negative experiences and tell foster kids that they won't succeed because of this. They should be teaching them the opposite. Foster children should know that because of these challenges, they will be stronger. They have been trained in a gauntlet of bad experiences to do better and face hard things and survive. They are tested and pushed, often experiencing horrors that most people can't imagine, but yet, when they make it through, they should know that they are strong. Most people would fold in the face of similar challenges. Use this knowledge and strength when you encounter new difficulties—that you have faced hard things before and will make it through whatever problems are up ahead.

I had seen Kiesha show this kind of strength, even when challenges knocked her down, but now I was learning it on my own. I was tiny but mighty. I started to use my gift of gab to stand up for myself and to snap back at the people who hurt me.

I also observed that most people would resort to insults when they were losing an argument. If I was arguing with someone and he didn't have the intelligence to articulate his perspective, he would start with the insults.

"Terrence, you are just saying that because you are a stupid crack-baby who no one wanted."

To me, this translated to, "Terrence, I am not smart enough to answer you intelligently, so I have to resort to insults that just prove that I am the stupid one."

This knowledge removed the power of whatever point that he was trying to make and immediately lowered his standing in my view. The insults stopped hurting as I realized that they were less about me and more about the shortcomings of the person using them.

The more I was insulted and stood up for myself, the stronger my skills of snapping back grew. If someone said something hurtful to me and I shredded him, it usually silenced him. He could bully when it made him feel bigger, but when someone stood up to him and tore apart his words, he didn't seem so big anymore.

I think that this is where some of my earliest comedy started. I was never going to be the biggest or baddest kid, but I was smart and quick-witted. I wouldn't pick on other people, but if they called me names or teased me, it was fair game for me to roast them right back. If someone taunted me, I usually had a fast reply that would cause everyone around them to cackle in laughter. Bullies would try to exploit my weaknesses, but I would play to my strengths. With each situation in which I snapped back, I grew in confidence. I learned not to be afraid of other people's verbal hits, but to stand firm and snap back.

Chapter Eleven

Adoption

She didn't know it then, but her own story of the American Dream was still being written.

When my mom would get us back, she would try to take care of us at first. Sometimes she would be clean for a little while, and sometimes she would be working, trying to prove to the courts that she could hold a steady job. When she could, she would sell plasma at a plasma center to gain a little bit of money. On one visit, as the nurse prepared my mom for her plasma donation, they began to talk. My mom mentioned to the nurse that she needed to find a daycare to send her children to. It turned out that the nurse had a sister named Tammy who ran a nearby daycare that had availability. My mom signed us up, and it was there that we met the owners, Tammy and Tony, for the first time.

We would go to their daycare on and off, and they grew increasingly familiar with our situation. When we were in Tammy and Tony's care, they watched over us as best they could, but they knew that we were facing severe challenges on all sides.

One day when we were at the daycare, Tammy pulled my siblings and me aside and told us that we would not be going with our mom that day. My mom had relapsed, and we would be going back into the system. The authorities would be arriving soon to pick us up. We all reacted differently. Some of my siblings cried. One of my brothers started running in circles, screaming before trying to make a sprint for the door. Out of all my memories of that daycare, this one stands out the most.

When we went back into foster care, this didn't end Tony and Tammy's investment in us. We saw them on and off, depending on whether we were with our mom or not, but they also recruited family members to help house us. Various members of Tammy's family fostered us at different times. She would try to find ways to watch out for us, even when we were in and out of the system. Eventually, I ended up with a cousin of Tammy's, while a brother and sister of mine stayed with Tony and Tammy. After a while, it was decided that it would be best if I joined my siblings and lived with their family.

By that time, I had been in and out of somewhere between eight and ten foster homes. My siblings had been shuffled around as much or more than I had. We would stay with our mom while she was doing well, but eventually we would always end up in the system. When she was not drugging and drinking, we could see my mom's love for us and soaked it in, but when the drugs took over, she just wasn't the same.

The final time that we were taken from my mom, she had been doing well. She had passed all her drug tests, and we were rooting for her. On the morning of her final court date, a surprise drug screen revealed that my mom had tested positive for drug use. At this point, the judge had enough. He terminated her rights completely. We no longer belonged to her in the eyes of the state.

My mom was devastated and heartbroken. She was mad and blamed the system. As we had grown up, she had blamed everyone but herself. She had birthed many children and felt that there should be more resources to pay for them. She needed housing and accused the government of not providing her a better housing situation. We were hungry, and she felt like we could be given more food allowances. She saw America as a land of handouts, where she was never given enough. She was bitter and angry at the government and country that she felt had let her down. She didn't yet realize that America was a land of opportunity, just waiting for her to accept responsibility and take control of her actions. She didn't know it then, but her own story of the American Dream was still being written.

My story was still unfolding, but it was about to take a turn that many in the foster care system never experience. Tammy and Tony wanted to adopt me, my sister Lanana, and my brother Trayvon. Sibling groups are difficult to find foster families for, let alone be adopted. The fact that three of us were being adopted into the same family when they already had two biological kids of their own was pretty incredible.

On the day of the adoption, we appeared before the judge. The judge asked me two questions. "Son, do you want to be adopted by this family?"

Without stuttering, I replied with a firm, "Yes."

"Do you want to change your last name?" the judge further questioned.

"No," I replied. My name was one of the only things that had stayed with me my whole life, and I wanted to keep it.

Just like that, we became part of a family again. At the time, I had been shuffled around so much that I don't think that I recognized the significance of it or the permanency that something like that meant. I was just grateful to be safe and secure, surrounded by people that I loved.

Chapter Twelve

Make Them Laugh

You can make people laugh while
making them listen.

I was sitting in one of my middle school classes when a stern-faced teacher called me into the hallway.

"Terrence, why are you running around the hallways making all that noise when you were supposed to be in class?" the teacher admonished.

"It wasn't me," I replied, knowing full well that it actually was.

"I know that it was you. We could hear you laughing. Nobody else has that laugh. You laugh out loud, and it carries all the way down the hall. You are not going to sit here and call me a liar," he replied.

"I don't want to call you a liar, but y'all are lying. It wasn't me," I deadpanned.

But I *was* the culprit. I knew it, and he knew it. My distinctive laugh had given me away. It wasn't just chatter that bubbled out of me; my laughter did, too. If I thought something was funny, then I couldn't keep it inside. My laughter spilled out loudly and would spread to other people. If I laughed, they would laugh, and a chain reaction would start that was contagious.

This drove most of my teachers crazy, but other teachers found it equally amusing. I wasn't a disrespectful kid, but I did question things that didn't make sense to me.

I was the kind of kid that if an adult asked, "Are you calling me a liar?" I would reply, "Yeah." Why would he be asking me if I thought he was a liar if he weren't sure about it himself? If someone didn't want my answer, then he shouldn't have asked me the question. There were things like that I would question and laugh about.

By middle school, I think that most people identified my laugh with me, but it wasn't the talk of the town. No one was saying, "Did you hear Terrence's laugh? That is the guy with the laugh." However, if they heard my laugh, they could always identify it as mine.

I made good grades, but I just talked a whole lot. My good grades didn't leave my teachers much room for complaint. I was a chatterbox and class clown, yet my grades were still stellar. My adopted parents weren't worried about my talking and joking as long as I did well in school, so if the teachers complained, it didn't change much of anything. Tammy and Tony were proud of the grades that I was earning.

There was one exception, though. I did fail PE once. In middle school and high school, I helped my adopted family out with their paper route. They had a considerable route, which helped their income. Every morning,

I would get up before sunrise to help bundle and deliver newspapers, earning five dollars a bundle for myself. I liked working hard, making money for myself.

The one drawback was that I would often be tired at school and would want to catch up on sleep when I could. PE seemed to be the perfect opportunity to sleep in class.

The coach told us at the start of the year, "I am not going to force you to do anything. If you want to participate, then do it, but if you don't, that is your choice."

"You are not going to force us to do anything?" I questioned. "So, if I want to go to sleep, I can go to sleep?" The coach reaffirmed what he said.

"Well, shoot, then I am going to go to sleep." I took this to mean that I could sleep in the bleachers every day during class and still make a good grade.

While everyone else was running around and getting dirty and nasty, I was sleeping. When everyone returned from class sweat-drench and smelly, I was keeping my scent together so I could ask a girl out at lunchtime or some such foolishness.

The coach said that I could sleep if I wanted to—I just didn't know that he was going to fail me for it. I ended up having to retake PE after that.

Overall, I wasn't willfully defiant for no reason. If I had ISS or "In-School Suspension," it was usually for talking too much.

If something didn't seem right to me, I questioned it. If I questioned it and it seemed unjust, I stood up to it. However, I usually did this in a joking manner.

When I was in middle school, I went to a really rough school. If Corn Pop had been to a school, it would have been Rogers Middle School in Oklahoma. At the time, Rogers Middle School (now an elementary school) was a breeding ground for gang members, drugs, and violence. To combat this, the school leaders put protective measures in place, including requiring school uniforms, installing metal detectors, performing searches when we entered the building, and not allowing standard backpacks.

Even though we were only in middle school, uniforms were assigned to prevent kids from associating with specific gang colors. We could wear whatever shoes we wanted, but we had to dress in button-up shirts that were white, black, or navy blue. We had to also wear dress pants in one of those three colors or khaki.

Our backpacks had to be either clear plastic or some mesh-like netting so that they could be seen through at all times. Each day, we would walk in and place our backpacks on the table while we waited our turn to go through the metal detector. We would watch as they would dump out our bags, sifting through each item to make sure that no drugs or weapons were hidden inside. They would even flip through the pages of the books to make sure that there were no knives stashed between the sheets. Once, one of my brothers was busted trying to smuggle in a knife to stab someone. As crazy as it sounds, this was standard for that school.

If our stuff cleared as contraband-free, they would make us take off our belts and direct us through the metal detectors. Kids got creative and would stash their drugs or knives around the school in outdoor hiding places. Back in those days, school shootings were not the primary concern as rarely would someone want to come in and shoot up the whole school. The violence was targeted and aimed at particular rivals instead of a broad swath of people. Although I didn't like navigating through all the layers of protection, I am thankful for them and all the administrators who kept our school safe. Thankfully, there were no shooting incidences on campus during my time there.

On the last day of school in my eighth-grade year, we were promised that we could wear street clothes. This was a big deal for me. I had already participated in my eighth-grade graduation and was looking forward to the Free Friday Street Clothes Day. Wearing my street clothes for my last day of school was something that I was pumped for. I had gotten new clothes for the occasion and was super excited to show them off.

Before this, a huge fight broke out, and over one hundred kids from our school were involved. It was gang-related, something to do with one of the Bloods. As punishment, the administration decided to take away our Free Friday Street Clothes celebration. I was angry and disappointed. Why were kids who were not involved in the fighting getting punished? I wanted to protest what I thought was unfair.

If I couldn't wear my new street clothes, I wasn't going to comply fully, either. I didn't agree with the decision and didn't want to go along with it. I wanted to make a stand, even if it meant acting the fool. I got a bucket of bleach, dipped my hand in it, and put bleach handprints all over my pants' dark fabric. I cut a hole down the back of my dress shirt and smaller holes throughout my pants. I put on one tennis shoe and one church shoe. I wore one sock up high with my pants tucked into it, and one sock rolled down. I was looking like a hot mess.

I got off the school bus, and my principal, Mr. Brown, took one look at me and said, "You look like a damn fool. Get inside."

People were laughing at me and pointing, saying, "Look at Terrence. He is so funny."

My principal was not so amused. Mr. Brown came into the cafeteria and said, "Terrence, come with me."

I said, "Why?"

"Because you look like a damn fool. You must have lost your mind coming up in here looking like a damn fool."

The entire cafeteria was laughing with me as I was escorted out. Mr. Brown decided that I needed to spend the rest of the day at home. It ended up being a win-win for me, because I stood up against what I thought was wrong, made everyone laugh, and got sent home from school early to start my summer.

Mr. Brown wasn't wrong. I was behaving foolishly. I also realized that humor could be a valuable tool to protest perceived wrongdoing, and that laughter can bring awareness in its own way. I could make people laugh while making them listen. I hadn't yet honed that skill, but I was becoming aware that humor is a tool and that laughter can teach us lessons.

Chapter Thirteen

Training Day

Each time I survived something rough, I learned from it, and I grew stronger.

Although my teachers couldn't get me to stop joking or talking, there was one person who was always listening, and that was my Heavenly Father, God. My relationship with Him would get me through all the hardships and challenges that I endured. He was always there and was always ready to hear my endless chatter as I reached out to Him in prayer.

I don't remember attending church with my mother. She is a believer now, but back then, drugs were where she placed her faith. However, every foster family that I ever stayed with went to church. Even the mean old crazy lady, Mrs. Scarborough, would take us to church. I guess it is true that even Satan recognizes the power of God.

Beginning with the Solomons, I started attending church, and in every foster home after that, the pattern continued. I would wear my nicest Sunday shoes and best clothes. I loved attending Sunday school and listening to the pastor preach the sermon. I memorized scripture, doing my best to live the words that I had been taught. I didn't always do that, but I tried. I read my Bible and tried to learn and know the nature of God.

During those dark times in my childhood, when I was filled with sadness or despair, I would talk to God. He truly was my best friend, as I could always talk to Him whenever my heart was hurting, and He listened. When people were hurting me, I could find safety in God. As my father had been out of my life since I was a baby, I found comfort in knowing that I had a Heavenly Father who always wanted me, loved me, and adored me. It gave me peace knowing that I meant enough to God that He chose me as His own and loved me no matter what. I was His child, and He loved me. There was nothing that I could do, or that could be done to me, that would remove me from His love.

I also realized that God made me exactly the way that He did for a purpose. Yes, I talked a lot, laughed, was curious, questioned things, and goofed around. These were annoying traits to have as a student in a teacher's classroom, but they were also traits that God had given me to use to glorify Him. I couldn't have known then the direction that God had for my life and how He planned to use it, but I was beginning to recognize that those traits or gifts could be positive if used correctly. Sometimes I think that as a society, we are too quick to try to discipline certain characteristics out of people instead of perceiving that if nurtured successfully, often those traits can become our greatest gifts.

My motor mouth was one of these traits that I now recognize is a gift, but at that time, I just knew that it was something that drove my teachers crazy. My laughter and ability to draw in a classroom full of kids may have been distracting, but it is something that God has used since to gather attention to many important things.

Even the hardship had its place. There were times when I couldn't understand how a loving God could let me go through so many horrible things, but now that I have some wisdom and maturity, I see it differently. Not that I don't still struggle with the concept when I am going through something hard—I do—but I can see it from a broader perspective. In my mind, all the hard stuff that I went through was like my own boot camp, my training day for something bigger.

Each time I survived something rough, I learned from it, and I grew stronger. This taught me resilience. Being shuffled around from place to place taught me adaptability. Being bullied, abused, and picked on taught me the power of standing up for others who are in similar situations, and it also taught me to stand up for myself. Being neglected and rejected by my birth father taught me about the unconditional love of my Heavenly Father.

There were many challenges that could be perceived as unfavorable, but God used them for good. Each of the bad things that happened in my life shaped me perfectly to be who God wanted me to be. They trained me to be a soldier in the army of Jesus Christ. I was refined by fire, but God was with me the entire way.

Not only am I thankful for these bad things because they made me who I am, but I am also grateful that I can reach out and relate to others who have gone through similar situations. Don't misunderstand; I do not wish those kinds of experiences on anyone, nor would I ever choose to have gone through them myself, but I am thankful that God used them for good in my life. I am grateful that I can give others hope and encouragement because of the hardships that I faced. All of those things made me who I am today, and I recognize the importance and significance of that.

Chapter Fourteen

Follower

I thought that hanging out with thugs would somehow make me tougher or harder.

My faith in God did not mean that I was the perfect angel. I was not; I still am not. In high school, I especially struggled with this. I know that God calls us to follow Him, but something else was calling me, leading me down a destructive path. My relationship with God was a solid foundation, but instead of building on this, I decided to go my own way.

In high school, I stayed busy, working at a hospital handing out food trays and going to school. I liked to make my own money so that I could be independent while also saving to buy my first car. I also participated in Taekwondo and Muay Thai boxing. Aside from that PE class that I failed, I worked hard to get good grades and do well in school.

Instead of following my faith, I tried to follow others. My school was full of gangbangers and thugs, and there was a time when I thought that maybe I wanted to be a thug, too.

Obviously, I was too small to ever be a real thug. Let's be honest. How intimidating do you think that tiny Terrence would have been as a gangbanger? Nobody would have taken me seriously had I tried to be threatening or intimidating.

I didn't see this, though. Just like the bullies who had picked on me to try to make themselves feel bigger, I thought that hanging out with thugs would somehow make me tougher or harder. I thought that hanging out in the projects would make me cooler, so instead of making my own way, I became a follower.

The first time that I ever saw someone get shot in real life was when I was about fifteen or sixteen. I was at a sweet-sixteen birthday house party. This was no Beverly Hills–style luxury sweet-sixteen with new cars and choreographed dances. This was a house party in the projects, complete with gangbangers, guns, alcohol, and drugs. The house was packed full of people, and I was just one kid in a swarm of teens.

A fight broke out, and before long, people were pushing and shoving, screaming and hollering, and throwing punches when the sound of gunshots rang out. Scared and confused, everyone scattered as best they could. I ran outside and crouched beside the passenger tire of a car for cover. In the chaos, no one could tell where the shots were coming from or who they were directed toward. We all just did our best to hunker down and avoid getting hit.

The house party had taken place in a duplex type of structure. While we all hid from the gunfire, a car pulled up into the driveway adjoined to the party house. Just a few feet away from where I was hunkered down, a bullet strayed into that car and directly through the head of the woman driving.

When the scene quieted, some friends and I ran over to the car to see how we could help. I was horrified as I looked into the driver's seat and was confronted by the body of a mother with her head blown partially off. It was haunting, a sight that nothing could have prepared me to see. Police were called as the screams of her children reverberated in my ears.

This young mom had nothing to do with the house party. Out driving with her three young kids, she had no idea that she would be shot to death as she pulled into her driveway. The kids had to be all under the age of five. They were screaming and sobbing, terrified and confused. These children were peacefully riding with their mom one minute and then covered in a spray of blood and brain matter the next. They didn't deserve this.

I was shocked and disturbed, quivering from anxious aftershocks. As people from the party scattered to escape or come to grips with the trauma, I also hid away. I didn't return home that night, too scared and shaken by what had happened. It was unusual for me to be stunned into silence, but I struggled to make sense of what had occurred.

This incident made me realize that I did not want to be a gang member. If violence was standard for gangbangers, then this was something that I wanted no part in. I didn't want to follow a gang into another violent situation. It was bad enough when rival gangs killed each other, but this was an innocent victim whose life was taken while children lost their mother, stripped away by senseless violence.

I decided that I did not want to become a gang member, but that did not mean that I wasn't playing the part of a follower. I was. Since I was funny and made people laugh, people always wanted me to hang around. The bad thing was that the people that I hung out with weren't usually good friends. They were smoking, drinking, and doing drugs, and I was doing the same.

After the house party and shooting, I was afraid to go to parties or places where gangbangers started fighting or violence. However, this did not mean that I stayed out of the projects. My friends were there, and I would follow them to do whatever type of activity they were doing. Often this meant smoking weed, underage drinking, or taking prescription drugs that most definitely were not prescribed to us. Unlike my birth parents, I wasn't addicted to drugs, and for the most part, I didn't even like them that much. I just was being a follower. I was doing what I thought everyone else was doing and making them laugh while participating.

My adoptive family did not approve of this kind of behavior, so I had to sneak around, telling them that I would be in one place when I was hanging out somewhere else. They had high expectations for me and always wanted the best future and outcome for me. Tony and Tammy didn't drink or smoke, expecting me not to do these things either. They wanted me to create a new path for myself rather than follow the example and heartbreak of my parents.

My adoptive family pushed me to become a leader and to make responsible decisions. This was contrasted by the fact that many other people would make excuses for me not to succeed or do my best. Since I had been in foster care, people didn't expect much from me in the sense of behavior or accomplishment. They held me to a lower standard because of what I had gone through. My adoptive family didn't accept this, though. They knew and modeled that anyone can achieve the American Dream, even someone like me.

It wasn't just Tony and Tammy that raised the bar for me. Their whole family rallied around me, showing that they cared by pushing me to be better.

One night, I headed out into a bad part of the Oklahoma City area called Dungee with a chip on my shoulder. Tammy didn't want me to go because she knew that I would get into trouble, but I left anyway. Upset, she called her sister Sharita and told her what was going on.

Sharita was the same sister that had introduced Tammy to my mom years before. A nurse and former sergeant in the military, she didn't play around.

"What do you mean Terrence is hanging out in the projects?" she asked disgustedly.

Tammy explained the problem and said that I would call, but she was not sure that I would or when I would be back.

"We'll see about that," Sharita replied and hustled off with her husband, Justin, to go find me.

Sharita was a force to be reckoned with. Beautiful and confident, she fought for what she believed. She had a soft spot for me and treated us all like family, whether adopted or not. Like Kiesha used to fight for me, Sharita was ready to stand up for me in a different way.

In an area known for gangsters and prostitution, her car pulled up in Dungee, and she didn't hesitate to search for me. I heard my auntie and her white husband walking through the streets, yelling, "Terrence! Terrence!" I wanted to melt into the ground. Her husband had been my martial arts coach and was tough as nails, but to have a white dude wandering through a black neighborhood yelling my name was humiliating. Here

I was, trying to be all tough and hard, and they show up to embarrass me like that. I was cursing before they even got close.

My Aunt Sharita cursed right back, "What are you doing? What in the hell? How are you going to disrespect your momma like that? Get your ass in the damn car!"

We scuffled, and she threw me into the car. As it started to pull away, I jumped out of the moving vehicle. "Get the hell away from me. I am not going anywhere with you!" I yelled.

Sharita was having none of it. She threw me into the car again and gave me a whooping. My embarrassment before was nothing compared to what I felt after being spanked soundly by my aunt.

People had stood up to bullies on my behalf, but my Aunt Sharita was standing up to me, saying, "This is enough." I didn't like it at the time, but I realize now that this was substantial.

Instead of just expecting me to fail or be a thug, some people loved me and saw that I could choose to be more. They expected me to lead and not to follow. They showed me that I wasn't defined by my past circumstances or confined by others' actions. I could do better. I could be different. I could grab the opportunities presented to me and make my own way. I could lead and live a life of purpose and direction.

Chapter Fifteen

Protection and Purpose

I could continue to be a follower and end up on a path to destruction, or I could learn to lead.

I may have pushed God aside for a time to be a follower of others, but He was still watching over me. He loved me and wanted me to follow Him.

In my childhood, there were so many times when I could have died from starvation, neglect, abuse, dehydration, gangbangers, or violence, yet through all of that, God kept me safe. It wasn't easy or smooth sailing, but He brought me through demanding situations and never left my side.

God blessed me in ways that I could have never predicted or imagined. One of these blessings in my early life had been the love of the Solomon family. When I was sent back to stay with my mom around second grade, I figured that the Solomons were gone from my life forever. I knew that they loved me and wanted me, but I hadn't seen them in years. I thought about them often and missed them, wondering what had happened to them.

During my freshman year of high school, I sat in English class with the most annoying kid in the world. If you thought that I talked a lot, you would have been astounded by this kid. He did not shut up. Due to my motor mouth, my teachers often sat me at the front of the classroom to keep me quiet. Usually, this worked well, because I didn't try to be disrespectful. In one class, they sat me in the very front row next to this endlessly obnoxious kid.

"Dude, shut up!" I warned him one day. He kept talking, ignoring my pleas for his silence. This kid just irked my nerves.

One day, as he talked, he pulled out a picture book. It was like a little photo album.

Then a photo caught my eye. "Hey, wait! Who's that?" I asked. "Are those your grandparents?"

"Yeah," he replied.

"Do they go by Maw-Maw and Paw-Paw?" I asked eagerly.

"Yeah, they do," he replied, slightly confused.

"Those are my Maw-Maw and Paw-Paw, too," I said excitedly. "Dude, I used to stay with them in foster care a long, long time ago."

"Oh," he said. "You are *that* Terrence. They always talk about you," he said, realizing that we had both met at the Solomons' house when we were young.

I asked where the Solomons were and what they had been doing, and he told me that I needed to call them. He gave me their number and assured me that they would love to hear from me. I had wondered about them and wished I could see them all those years, and in God's perfect way of working things out, I had been assigned a seat in class next to their grandchild.

I made the phone call that night and was thrilled when Maw-Maw answered.

"Ooooh... child, what in the world is going on?" Maw-Maw answered the phone, her voice quivering with excitement. "How did you get my number, baby?" she asked.

I explained the situation.

"Oh, John, John, it's Terrence! Oh, child, we have been looking for you all these years. We think about you all of the time, baby," her joy came brimming to the surface.

Paw-Paw got on the line, and soon I heard, "Clarence. Oh, Clarence, my boy! It is so good to hear from you," his emotions spilling over into the phone.

Paw-Paw's health was in decline at the time as he had dementia, but he still remembered me. They were so thrilled to hear from me. We swapped stories of the years since I left their care, and they told me about how they tried to get me back.

Wanting to see me, they sent me a Greyhound bus ticket, and that summer, I went to visit them for a month. I don't know what home feels like for most people, but for me, the Solomons felt like home. Maw-Maw greeted me with tears in her eyes and emotion in her voice. Paw-Paw was all "Clarence this," and "Clarence that."

Paw-Paw was retired, and his dementia waned and waxed, causing his clarity and memory to do the same, but he was just as hard-working and motivated as ever. If I thought the summertime was for sleeping in, I was wrong.

"Clarence, get up. I don't believe in a man sleeping past nine. You come to help me, boy. There is work to be done. You can't be sleeping all day," Paw-Paw chided. "I know that you are here to visit, but you are going to work. You gotta learn, you gotta learn."

Paw-Paw was supposed to be retired, but despite Parkinson's, dementia, and other health issues, he was a whirlwind of activity, putting us to work on various projects around their house and their property.

The Solomons were pleased that my speech had improved so much. I still stuttered, but they had been persistent with my therapy when I was little and were thrilled that it had diminished so much over the years.

When the Solomons took me back to the bus station at the end of the visit, Paw-Paw jumped out of the car and proudly stopped strangers saying, "This is my grandson, Clarence."

He beamed. "Clarence, look here. This here is my boy, Clarence."

He glowed with joy as he introduced me with love to stranger after stranger. Even in the throes of dementia, he showed me how proud that he was of me. Although slightly embarrassing at the time, this was also meaningful. A few months after my visit, Paw-Paw passed away. I am so grateful that God worked things out so I was able to spend time with him and reconnect, making special memories.

I don't believe that it is an accident that I was assigned a seat by the annoying kid who talked too much in my ninth-grade English class. I know that God perfectly planned it to reconnect me with the Solomons.

I also believe that God was watching over me and protecting me in ways far greater than I had imagined. He placed people in my life who adopted me, stood up for me, and watched over me. I know that He also had angels surrounding me.

An incident when I was around eighteen or nineteen demonstrated the Lord's protection over my life. I was not hanging out with gangbangers, but I still was struggling with being a follower. Instead of thinking independently, I was trying to fit in with everyone else. This meant that I was still hanging out with bad people and going to bad places. I wasn't using my God-given thoughts and intelligence to make wise decisions.

One evening, two of my friends loaded into my raggedy black 2002 Chevy Impala. We headed off to a concert, driving through the east side of Oklahoma City, which was an area known for gangs and violence. As we drove, the car shuddered, and we heard a loud, unfamiliar noise.

"I think something just hit your car," my friend said, turning in his seat to look out the rear window.

"What you mean?" I said, lowering the volume on my radio, looking around and trying to see what he was talking about.

"No, dude, I think that someone is shooting at your car," he said this time with a terrified look in his eyes.

"What you talking about?" I said, searching out my review mirror.

Behind us was an old dark green Honda Civic, and a guy was hanging out of the window shooting at us. I did my best to duck and drive, but the car kept chasing us as bullets whizzed by around us. Terrified, I slammed my foot down on the accelerator, trying my best to speed away. The Honda tried to get closer, pulling up beside me and shooting into the car. I swerved and weaved and did everything that I could to try to pull away.

As we neared a light, the Civic made a fast u-turn and drove straight toward us, spraying my car with bullets. Shaking, I sped off before pulling into a parking lot to take stock of what had happened. Miraculously, I was unharmed, and both of my passengers were scared, yet unscathed.

My car was not so lucky. The tires were shot out, bullets had gone through both headlights, and there were bullets in various parts of the vehicle. The driver's door had a shot go through it and drop down lower into the car. Had the bullet continued its trajectory, it would have hit me in the stomach or ribs and killed me. Another round stopped by the vehicle was traveling straight toward my head. Incredibly fortunate, I was confident that angels had shielded me in that car.

My friends both had marijuana in the car, so we decided not to call the police. Shaken, I called my brother to pick me up and had the car towed the next day. This incident was a wake-up call for me, and I realized that I needed to live life differently. My car had become a target, not because of me, but because of the people that I hung around. Most likely, some gang members had spotted my car when I was hanging out in the projects and associated me with some rivals. Following the wrong leaders was a dangerous path leading to sorrow.

I recognized that I needed to make a change. I could continue to be a follower and end up on a path to destruction, or I could learn to lead. I could see God's hand of protection over me, but I knew that He was calling me in a different direction than the one I had headed down.

God protected me for a purpose. It was my responsibility to fulfill that purpose.

Chapter Sixteen

Made for More

God had made me for a purpose,
and I needed to fulfill that.

"Terrence, I don't usually tell people this, and I don't want you to take it the wrong way," my teacher said. "You go to college and do whatever you are planning on doing, but do not waste your time behind a desk. You have a personality that needs to be out in front of the world."

I considered her words as I packed up my stuff and prepared to attend Rose State College. My adoptive family emphasized getting a college education. I loved learning, so college seemed to be a natural next step for me. The college had a program that allowed me to go to school tuition-free for two years, so I capitalized on that.

Attending college also allowed me to slowly fade away from some of the bad influences that I had surrounded myself with, and I knew that this was important. I was still enmeshed with people making bad decisions, and this gave me a chance to break away, following the natural course of action that moving and changing bring over time.

I worked, attended classes, and tried to stay out of trouble. I loved learning, but the more I attended classes, the more I felt that I was wasting my time. I had always been a quick study, and it frustrated me that my professors were spending so much time on concepts that I felt could be covered more quickly if I read about them myself. The lectures were not merely a presentation of material with a creative exchange of ideas and information. Rather, a professor would lecture on something and then told us what to think about it. I didn't like this. It didn't matter if I had a different perspective or way of viewing things. If I wanted to get a good grade, I had to agree with the stream of thought presented. I think that for many college students, this blind way of following is a relief during a critical time when they are making so many decisions on their own, but for someone like me who naturally questioned and was curious, this was difficult.

I began reading and studying the coursework on my own before switching to classes online. I still maintained good grades, performing well on assignments and tests, but I was growing disillusioned and restless. I knew that college was an important rite of passage, but the words of my high school teacher kept ringing in my ear: "Do not waste your time behind a desk. You have a personality that needs to be out in front of the world."

I felt that I was made for more, yet I was wasting time. I valued education and knew it was necessary, but deep within me was a calling for something greater. God had made me for a purpose, and I needed to fulfill that. College is right for many people, but it was time for me to go in a new direction.

My mantra is that there is no point in stressing about something that I can't change. If I can change something, there is still no point in stressing about it; I should just change it. This was one of those defining moments.

There were so many things in my life that I couldn't change. I couldn't erase the neglect, the abuse, the starvation, or the abandonment in the foster care system, so I chose not to stress about these things. There were things that I could change. Instead of wallowing in my dissatisfaction with my college experience, I decided to change it. Instead of stressing others' expectations or following a more traditional path, I chose to pursue the talents that God had given me and push forward in a different direction.

I knew that I had a personality that made others laugh and that people responded well to me, so I decided to focus on the abilities that God had given me and pursue a career in acting and entertainment. My dream was to make it big one day in Hollywood while helping other kids from the foster care system succeed. However, I also recognized that chasing dreams meant hard work and diligence. If I wanted to become an actor, I had to train to be one. I had to build a foundation to stand on. Just like with my faith, I had to invest time and effort to grow.

Although acting successfully in Hollywood was my dream, I had to be realistic. I was just a kid from Oklahoma, and although I was working nonstop, I didn't have the finances to make a move straight to LA. I couldn't change that, so I didn't stress over it. The thing that I could change was leaving college and making a step toward that new future. Hollywood was still my goal, but to get there, I knew that I needed to continue making steps forward in whatever way that I could.

Moving to Austin, Texas, was my next step. When I lived in Oklahoma, every time I looked for acting jobs, the closest ones were in Austin. The capital city of Texas, Austin was only about a six-hour drive from my family. I decided that this would be a great place to start. I found a job there and a small apartment with a roommate. Determined to succeed, I lined up as many acting classes as I could squeeze in between working hours. I wasn't afraid of hard work and wanted to develop my natural gifts.

In between acting classes and working, I scheduled auditions, but nothing significantly paid off. I kept moving forward, pushing to be better while searching for opportunities. I didn't care where I started. I just wanted to entertain. I was from humble beginnings, so working my way up was something that I was eager to do. For almost an entire year, I pounded the pavement, trying to find an acting job, only to be continuously rejected. I took each rejection as an opportunity to learn and kept preparing.

Eventually, I saw that the reality television show, *Big Brother*, was holding auditions in Austin. I knew absolutely nothing about the show, but I thought that it might be an excellent chance to break into television and collect a more substantial paycheck. I stood in line to audition with throngs of other people.

More casting call than audition, the producers brought us into a room in groups and asked us a bunch of questions. Everyone in my group had extensive knowledge of the show, reciting trivia and facts about nearly everything. I knew nothing. I had never even watched an episode. When the casting director got to me, she asked why I was there.

"To be honest with you, I'm just here to make some money and get on TV," I said jovially. "I don't even know if I qualify... I... I... I just want to get some of that money that you are passing out." I stuttered out an answer that caught the casting director off-guard.

Amused, she said, "You didn't watch the show before you came?"

I replied earnestly, "No, I didn't really care to watch the show. I just want to be on it. Is that okay?"

She laughingly chided, "Well, you are trying to win some money, so you have to know about the show."

"Well, okay then," I replied.

I wasn't trying to be funny when I said it, just truthful, but I think that it caught her off-guard and amused her. To be honest, I never thought that I would get a callback, but I did. The callback led to some Skype interviews, and when I shared my foster care story during the meetings, it caught their attention. She told me that she was moving me forward to the next round.

"Look," she said. "I am moving you to the next round and bringing you to California. Your personality is wonderful, and people are just going to gravitate around you. Your story is amazing, and you are so joyful even after going through such hard stuff."

I was so excited that this might be my big break. I flew out to California and went through the arduous meetings with casting directors and producers as they narrowed down the final contestants to be placed in the *Big Brother* house. In the end, they didn't choose me, but they did make me an alternate cast member in case something went wrong with someone inside the house and needed to drop out.

I was assigned handlers to assist me as I went through the process. These individuals were usually other people involved in the industry in some way, assisting or trying to make a break for themselves. Day in and day out, I spent significant time with my handlers.

"Dude, I don't know why they didn't pick you to put you in," said one of my handlers. "That is so sad that you didn't get to make it, but your personality is amazing. You are going to be a star one day. I can see it," he assured me.

Within a week, these words came true as I went viral with my first Facebook Live video.

Chapter Seventeen

Going Viral

I had grown up witnessing this victimhood mentality my whole life, but it never rang true to me.

One year after moving to Austin, my career as an entertainer was not moving forward as I had envisioned. I had been working hard, yet had not landed a substantial opportunity. I kept pushing forward. The chance to be on *Big Brother* had not panned out, but I knew that eventually doors would open.

About that time, political rhetoric was heating up as our country moved into the 2016 election season. I would go on my personal social media pages and see my friends bickering back and forth about politics. Growing up, I was told that I was a Democrat, but I never took it too seriously. In my mind, I wasn't defined by a political party. I was just Terrence, an individual who thought freely. When I talked about politics with friends, they always assumed that because I was black and grew up in foster care or the projects, I should think a certain way or associate with the Democratic Party. My life experiences had taught me otherwise. I questioned things that other people blindly accepted, and I challenged ideas on both sides of the aisle that I didn't agree with.

I never thought that my beliefs were all that different than anyone else's. I just had what I thought was a practical way of looking at things, so I questioned it when others did not.

One day, I kept seeing friends posting nonsense, saying things like, "Terrence, let's move back to Africa."

Move back? Excuse me? I have never even been to Africa. I am from Oklahoma. Why would I move "back" to a country that I was never part of in the first place? It didn't make any sense. I felt blessed to be in America, the land of opportunity, yet here my black friends wanted to leave the country that I was proud of to go to a land that had sold its ancestors off as slaves to make a profit. There was no logic in their thinking. They wanted handouts, yet they proposed going to a society where there would be no handouts. This seemed nonsensical.

My friends weren't African. They were American, yet they were utterly ungrateful for the endless opportunities this country presented them. It reminded me of my friends from the projects. Throughout my childhood, they were always angry that the government wasn't helping more. When the government gave them more, it was never enough. They embraced victimhood, railing that they needed more food stamps, better housing, and more resources. This victimhood mentality enslaved them to the government and the handouts that it gave. The political party that provided the most handouts was the party that was supported. There was no personal responsibility, just blame. Opportunity was wasted, replaced with bitterness and feeling of entitlement.

I had grown up witnessing this victimhood mentality my whole life, and it never rang true to me. I could have claimed a greater sense of victimhood than my mom did. After all, I had been abused, neglected, left starving, and stripped of responsible parents—abandoned to the system. Yet, I was not a victim. Yes, those things happened and were beyond my control, but this was America where young men and women can dream big dreams and achieve greater success. I was made to thrive, and to do this, I accepted that my faults, failures, and poor decisions were my own. The things that I didn't like and couldn't control, I didn't stress over. Stressing would have held me back. I could change my outcome and would never buy into a system that told me otherwise. I would not be held as a slave to the control of victimhood.

These thoughts, combined with hunger, drove me to hit Facebook Live while I ate my lunch in the car that day. I was hungrily devouring my fried chicken when I read some posts on my Facebook feed that struck me wrong. This particular day, I noticed the Facebook Live feature and decided to try it out. I ate my chicken while speaking my mind.

I thought that the video was honest and funny, but not anything exceptional. I expected a few friends to comment, laugh, or roll their eyes and say, "That's Terrence for you, always giving his opinion."

I had no idea that post would go viral, but somehow it did. I was shocked as I watched the number climb steadily for days as people shared it, posted it, tweeted it, and retweeted it. My post snowballed beginning with a few likes and shares, and then it gained momentum as it was shared hundreds, then thousands, and now, millions of times. I would have never predicted that reaction. In retrospect, I think that people were looking for someone stating common sense ideas in a world so full of outrage and the victim mentality.

Many others felt the same way as messages of support and agreement poured in. There were also a lot of haters. I was accused of being racist for eating my lunch, which happened to be my favorite, fried chicken. As someone that was told by the Left my whole life that black people couldn't be racist, the irony was that those same people were slamming me and accusing me of the very facts that they denied.

The interesting thing was that my post hadn't been political. I didn't mention either party. I didn't say the words "conservative" or "Democrat." I just stated my way of common sense thinking, and this resonated with people on both sides, but overwhelmingly on the conservative side. This was eye-opening to me. Here I was just speaking the truth that should have made sense to anyone. Yet, the Democrats wanted to suppress it, capitalizing on the use of victimhood that they had skillfully orchestrated as the party of slavery, the KKK, the modern-day plantation of the projects, race-baiting, the 90s crime bill that further enslaved black America, and more.

The Democratic Party had done nothing for me except try to turn me into a victim. They thought that the scraps of public assistance that they handed out should earn them unending loyalty within the black community, and anyone who questioned this would be attacked with seething hatred and threats. For speaking out, I was called racist, a sell-out, a tap-dancer for the white man, and far worse for simply voicing my personal nonpartisan ideas. I questioned the status quo and was raked across the coals for it by Democrats.

All my life, I had been told, "Terrence, don't be a follower; don't be a follower," but when I acted on this advice, I was met with derision and hatred.

The flip side to that was all the support that I received from everyone else. I was lovingly embraced and encouraged by those who supported my rights to free speech and independent thinking. I quickly grew a following of people who loved that I questioned the traditional narrative and spoke my thoughts about it. This didn't mean that my followers agreed with everything that I said, but that, in itself, was good. They recognized that our experiences shape our perceptions, and we can view things and evaluate things for ourselves, agreeing on some topics and disagreeing on others. It is healthy to have differing opinions and to share them in a constructive or even humorous way, learning and growing as we listen to other people's points of view. It is also healthy to be able to question things that don't seem right to us and not just blindly accept that there is only one way to view something or one Party to follow blindly.

I continued to post videos as my viewership grew. I gained thousands of new followers on my various social media platforms each day as people liked and shared my videos. I read and educated myself on the topics and grew stronger with certain convictions while letting go of others that had been drilled into me from childhood. I knew for sure that I wasn't alone in my beliefs; there were multitudes of people who were sick and tired of the media or government telling them how to think and what to follow.

Successful businessman Donald J. Trump and former United States Secretary of State and First Lady Hillary Clinton faced off in the 2016 election. When I posted my first video, I had no idea that it would resonate in the current political climate, cresting as it inspired a new wave of people who were disillusioned with career politicians and power players. Hillary Clinton was a lifelong politician who had been in power when many of the oppressive policies aimed at black America had been put into place. Donald J. Trump was a wild-card. No one had expected him to push to the front of the pack, but he did, and he was driving forward with impressive power toward the presidency. Just as I had learned in life not to be a follower, here came Trump blazing his own path, refusing to follow others, and standing up for our country. He reminded our Nation that this is indeed the greatest country in the world. Successful in business, he was unapologetically himself. For better or for worse, you knew that with Trump, you would get a free thinker who couldn't be bullied by either party into accepting ideas that didn't make sense or work for America. Trump wanted to make America great again and was willing to fight for the ideals on which this country was founded. This was refreshing, and it no doubt got President Donald J. Trump elected into office.

It is interesting to me that people assume that since I am black and grew up in foster care, I would automatically want to be a Democrat. Why would I embrace the mentality that I saw hold so many other people in bondage? Why would I want to be told how to think when I can think for myself? Why would I want to depend on the government to live when America has given me the opportunity to make my own way? The American Dream is not poverty and the projects. The American Dream is not victimhood and handouts. The American Dream is not subjugation and suppression of free speech and thought. The American Dream is the freedom to succeed and thrive, blossoming in the gifts and abilities that God has endowed within us. I believe in this beautiful Nation that God has given us. Life, liberty, and the pursuit of happiness are the things that make our Nation great.

The wool had been pulled over our eyes for far too long, but people were waking up to the truth. As my popularity online grew, some of my friends and family expressed concern. Although I had never called myself a conservative, I found that my beliefs labeled me as one. I was cautioned that this would make things difficult for me within the black community, but most people respected that I always had my own views and supported me in that.

My family did not necessarily agree with my political views, but even they realized the truth of the American Dream. My birth mother, who had taken from others her whole life and had nothing to show for it but pain and heartache, was making changes. After losing her children to the system, she stopped using drugs. She still struggled with alcohol use, but after the birth of my youngest brother, Rayvon, she realized that she had better sober up or she would lose him, too. She began making baby steps toward healing and accepting that she was responsible for her behavior. As she stopped blaming others and the system, she realized that she was free to make a new future on her own effort and strength. The government had failed her, but not in the ways that she initially thought. It had incentivized her not to marry, not providing stable father figures or a family structure for us. The money that it gave her never helped her to get ahead; it bound her to a system of reliance. Instead of working, it taught her that the less she made, the more she could get. Even if she maxed out what the government gave her, it would never be enough. Like slaves who thought they couldn't survive without a master, my mom was chained to the scraps of government assistance. She was bound by reliance and self-doubt, squelching the challenge of working hard and achieving on her own, gaining a sense of pride. She thought that her survival depended on that pittance, not realizing that with hard work and ambition, she could make far more than anything that the government could give her.

As she lived with sobriety, her mind cleared of drugs and alcohol, she realized that she had the responsibility and the power to do better. Ashamed at having let her children down, she determined to improve. She could tell us a million times that she was clean and sober, but we needed to see action and effort. We had seen her cycle through promises of a better life, only to crawl back to drugs and leave us to suffer. She understood this and wanted to prove that she could be a mother and grandmother for all of us to be proud.

It was a slow process, but she worked hard to start over. She grew closer to the Lord, accepting His forgiveness while hoping for the forgiveness of her children. She desperately wanted to make things right with her kids. She had hurt us terribly, but she felt that if God knew every despicable thing that she has ever done and forgave her, we would be able to forgive her in time. She embraced responsibility for the hurt that she caused and endeavored to do better.

She enrolled at Rose State College, the very college that I had left. She determined to make a difference for herself, for her legacy, and her own story. She knew that this brave step would cause healing and change generations to come. In the past, she had tried to go back to school several times but would give up when she didn't have transportation or struggled to make it to class. This time, there were no excuses.

"I didn't put the effort in," she acknowledged about past attempts, accepting that she would always be able to offer excuses, but excuses would never earn an achievement.

I am so proud of my mom because, despite her past, she changed to build a better future. At fifty-eight years old, my mom was glowing with the news that she graduated in 2020 with an Associate in Arts (AA) degree and is continuing her education to gain a license in nursing. If this is not the American Dream, then I don't know what is.

It wasn't just my video that was going viral; people were awakening everywhere to find freedom by casting aside victimhood and embracing personal responsibility. No longer prisoners of a system meant to enslave and bind, voices like mine were rising and speaking out.

Chapter Eighteen

Mentors

*I wasn't afraid of working hard and
sacrificing to build success.*

fter I went viral, my viewership continued to grow. I continued to make videos and was surprised that my following continued to abound. Sometimes I said things that resonated, and equally, I offended people, but I remained true to my beliefs and tried not to let bullies bother me or dissuade me. A follower no longer, I set out to lead on a path paved with wisdom.

After I went viral, I got the word that my biological dad, whom I hadn't seen since I was a child, had resurfaced. For so many years, I wondered about him, not knowing if he were dead or alive or why he had never made an effort to contact me or connect. Now was my chance to find out. I arranged to meet him, not knowing what he looked like or how I would recognize him. Our meeting was not one out of a Hallmark movie. There were no tears or turning points. It was brief and emotionless. We went our separate ways, and that was that.

One of the biggest challenges in our nation, but particularly in the black community, is fatherless families.

A good dad can make a world of difference in a child's life, and statistics attest to this. An absent or harmful dad can sow seeds of destruction. My biological dad wasn't there to mold or shape me positively, but God placed other mentors and father figures in my life to guide me along. John Solomon was one of these figures. My adoptive dad, Tony, was another. My Heavenly Father never left me and has provided people to step up and stand in that role. It wasn't just father figures that God lovingly surrounded me with; he also gave me mentors to teach me how to lead. Following bad people will get you into trouble. Following wise leaders will help you to grow.

The year *Big Brother* had chosen not to cast me, I went viral shortly after. As another year rolled around, I heard from *Big Brother* again. They told me that they would like to put me on their show and that no audition was necessary. I was excited to finally get my chance to be on national TV, moving toward becoming an entertainer.

Unexpectedly, I received an email from *Big Brother* producers informing me that I was no longer being considered for the show. No real explanation was given; I was out. I was disappointed but figured that God had a plan, even in this. He most definitely did. Within a week, I was in a dialogue with Sean Hannity.

Sean Hannity, a conservative commentator on the nationally syndicated radio talk show *The Sean Hannity Show* as well as the Fox News program *Hannity*, had followed me on Twitter. He had liked and retweeted a post of mine, leading to dialogue in which I thanked him. To my delight and surprise, he invited me to do a segment on his show every day for one week called "The Last Word." It was a brief segment in which I shared my views in pre-recorded clips, but the exposure that I got was positive and increased my social media presence.

It was both surprising and humbling, but the biggest blessing from it was Hannity's kindness and support. Brilliantly accomplished, he took the time to talk with me and mentor me like a true friend. He encouraged me that I needed to try standup comedy and gave me advice on the steps that I should take. Not only that, but if I ever had a question or needed to talk with him, he availed himself to me wholeheartedly, giving me his time and wisdom. I had never met him in person, but yet, he welcomed me in as a friend. I had been banking on *Big Brother*, but realized that in not giving me that show, God gave me something better. He gave me a brother and mentor in Sean Hannity.

Inspired by Sean, I aspired to succeed in comedy. I tried to book opportunities at various comedy clubs or venues, but I was repeatedly turned down and was told that I had to be an established comedian to perform at those establishments. Undeterred, I decided to create my own opportunity. I sold some of my belongings to raise some money and rented a venue, advertising myself. I wasn't afraid of working hard and sacrificing to build success.

My first show did well, but I lost some money and learned in the process, getting better each time I performed. Each comedy show allowed me to entertain, but it also gave me the power to do something significant and to give back. In each city that I went to, I would partner with a local non-profit that worked with kids from foster care and would use my performances to help them raise money for the kids. I wanted to bless and inspire other kids like me and use the platform that God gave me to do some good for others. I knew that making money through entertaining would never be enough for me; I wanted to do more. I desired to use the gifts that God had given me to help kids in foster care in whatever way I was able.

Appearing on *Hannity* and continuing to make viral videos on social media allowed me to reach more people, but within that, there was a lot of negativity. I was constantly threatened and began receiving death threats. Some of the vilest messages that I received were from people that I used to be friends with, angered that I would dare form my own opinions and think for myself. For years, the liberals had pushed a platform of false tolerance, not extending this same tolerance to anyone with views that didn't match their own. If I didn't get in line with what black Americans were told to believe, then I was a threat who needed to be brought down. It was a disturbing way of thinking.

Tired from the constant stream of menacing messages, after repeatedly appealing to the social media platforms with no action taken, I set about to expose those making the threats by sharing them. I would post the threatening or hateful messages along with a brief message where I snapped back in a humorous way. Instead of being protected from those harassing and intent on harm, these platforms responded by censoring me.

Despite this, my audience grew, eventually reaching followers in the millions. I was humbled and grateful that so many Americans and people all over the world would connect with me through my pages.

Each person that follows me is a blessing. I am still in awe that so many people listen to what I have to say and laugh along with me in my posts. One day, I noticed Lara Trump was following me, and my jaw just about hit the floor. She was the first member of the Trump family to follow me, and I couldn't believe it. I nearly had a heart attack—or maybe it was heartburn from overeating fried chicken—but either way, I was stunned. I reached out to her, thanking her for following me and expressing how much it meant to me.

On a visit to New York City, I reached out to many friends and acquaintances to meet up. Most were too busy or blew me off. Lara Trump and Lynn Patton cleared their busy schedules to take me to breakfast. This spoke volumes to me about their character. I had actual friends there that were too busy to meet with me, yet Lara and Lynn, who are both incredibly accomplished and who maintain rigorous work schedules, carved out time to meet me. We had breakfast together, and I was in awe of the kindness and care they demonstrated.

As if I had not already taken enough of her time, Lara invited me back to Trump Towers for a tour and to meet her husband, Eric Trump. While helping to run the international enterprise Trump Organization, Eric invested his time in me, a seemingly random internet comedian. Eric and Lara made time for me when other people didn't. They were so genuine and kind, going above and beyond to make me feel welcome. I would love to think that I got some sort of special red carpet treatment, but it was evident that they treat all they welcome in with care. This is something that I respect and admire deeply about them.

It was interesting that "friends" were sending me death threats, accusing the Trump family of being elitist and racist, while the Trumps went above and beyond to show love and kindness, going out of their way to welcome me in. This spoke volumes to me about their character and left a lasting impression.

I was still posting regular videos on my social media platforms while I grew my comedy. Additionally, I was still auditioning for various projects. I was working nonstop to make a better life for myself, and in doing so, I encouraged other foster care children that there was hope for them.

Once again, it seemed that I was about to get a big break. A new Netflix TV show that I had auditioned for decided to cast me in a supporting role. This wasn't reality TV; this was an actual acting job. This show was an opportunity that I had dreamed about doing. It would be filmed in Bangkok, Thailand, and it would be a whole new adventure for me. I was thrilled.

Then, the filming schedule came out. My role was required to film at the same time as a comedy show scheduled in December of that year. If this had been just a regular comedy show, I could have canceled it and refunded the tickets. However, this was not a regular show; it was far more important. For months, volunteers had been working around the clock for my show, which doubled as a charity event to raise money to provide shoes for children in foster care. The show was about so much more than an opportunity for me; this was a life-changing chance to bless kids in foster care.

I spoke to the director of the Netflix show to see if I could get the timing changed, but the production schedule was set and could not be altered. They had to stick to the plan. The director told me that if I kept the role, I would make a lot more money that could be used to help the children. He tried to convince me that I would make far more money and impact by filming than with the comedy show fundraiser. He was right in that I would have made more money to donate to the kids, but sometimes it is about more than money; it is about doing what is right. I had committed to these kids and needed to fulfill that. Foster kids are used to being brushed aside, their value minimized. I wasn't going to do this to them. I was a mentor to these children—the actions that I took were setting an example. I made a commitment and determined to honor that. I gave up my role and trusted that just as God had provided for my good in other seasons of disappointment, He would work this situation out for His glory.

Once again, disappointment led to a dream fulfilled. Although I had given up the role in the Netflix show, something else materialized. A group of conservative comedians and commentators, including myself, joined together in what would be approximately a thirty-city tour at venues across America.

This tour, branded The Deplorables Tour and pro-duced by Max Gottlieb, was scheduled for 2019, and the name was in reference to Hillary Clinton's attack that Trump supporters belong in a "basket of deplorables." Embracing the insult was a way of snapping backing in a tongue-in-cheek way at her derogatory rhetoric.

This tour was an excellent opportunity to use my motor mouth for good, encouraging people all across America to think for themselves and to stand up to the status quo. It also meant that I could make people laugh, and I loved making people laugh.

At the beginning of 2019, our shows began, and I was thrilled to be a part of such a great tour, diving full force into stand-up comedy. Things were starting to take off, and I reveled in doing something that I loved, entertaining.

Chapter Nineteen

The Crash

As I struggled through surgery and the grueling recovery, He brought light into my life through my fans.

If having Lara Trump follow me on Twitter gave me heart palpitations, then getting the news that I was invited to an event at the White House for National African American History month just about left me dead. I couldn't believe it. I was going to the White House.

I missed my flight into DC and had to rapidly reschedule, flying into Baltimore-Washington International Airport instead of Reagan as initially planned. I had scheduled a car service to pick me up, take me to a barber for a haircut, and then drop me off at the hotel as I prepared to go to the White House.

We left the airport, the driver weaving his way through the sea of glowing tail lights, braking and shifting through Washington, DC, traffic. I was too excited to concentrate, scrolling through my social media, and excitedly texting various friends, overjoyed that I was going to be a guest at the White House. I grew up without a permanent house, and here I was, invited to be a guest of the president of the United States. Butterflies didn't just dance in my stomach; they were full-out boxing as my eagerness grew.

As I flipped through my phone, I felt the vehicle swerve. I looked up in time to see us sliding toward a bridge, and I thought that this was the end. Gripping tightly to the door handle, the words, "OH SHIT!" flew from my mouth as the car spun three hundred and sixty degrees before stilling with a jolting crash. It all happened so quickly, yet somehow, my brain flipped through a hundred different scenarios as if the few seconds in time were preserved in slow motion.

It felt as if I had been hit by a train. Cars behind us screeched to a sudden stop, their tires squealing in protest. Flying forward in my seat, my head had slammed into the window. I slumped over, not wanting to move. My head throbbed, white lights spinning above me. I felt as if I could fall asleep and never wake up.

Get up, Terrence. You have to get up! I felt that if I stayed there, I would die, and I didn't want to die.

I pulled myself up and out of the car, the pain so excruciating that I almost passed out. The driver helped me stagger away from the wreckage. I was stunned; the pain in my body was screaming, but around me, I could hear nothing except an aggravating ringing in my ears. Everything felt broken. Everything hurt. My neck ached, I was scorched with pain, and my chest was growing tight, making it difficult to draw in a breath.

I felt as if my body were filled with thousands of glass shards trying to force their way out through my skin. The pain overwhelmed me as I was escorted by ambulance to a nearby hospital.

The news about my accident spread fast—probably because I tweeted about it. In all fairness, my fingers weren't broken, just my neck. I was in the ER overnight as the physicians ran tests, x-rays, and an MRI, revealing that I had fractured my neck and injured my spine. The damage was significant, and the doctors informed me that I would need to have surgery to fix my neck. I was admitted to the hospital, unable to move from my hospital bed. Placed on a liquid diet that I drank through a straw, I couldn't even get up to relieve myself. I was stuck on my back, secured with a neck brace. I languished in my hospital room while doctors decided on the best plan of action.

Immediately, support for me came pouring in. Friends from the event that I was supposed to be attending stopped by to offer support and encouragement; fans flooded my feed and inbox with messages of prayer and hope; and even though the situation was bleak, I found joy and laughter.

It was discouraging, though. Life had been speeding forward, and I had been beyond pumped about my comedy tour and going to the White House to meet the president when it all came crashing down. Thankfully,

I had health insurance to cover the bills, but this was a huge setback. I wanted to wallow in self-pity, but I also knew that God was faithful and that somehow things would work themselves out. I had made it through hard things before, and I would make it through this, becoming stronger in the process.

Then, Sean Hannity called. He had heard what happened and wanted to help. Hannity told me not to worry about my tour or anything except healing. He said, "Whatever you need, I got you. Just focus on healing. Be comfortable and heal the best you can."

I was overwhelmed by his support. This wasn't empty rhetoric; Hannity immediately took action, introducing me to the best surgeon in the state who would operate on me, fixing my neck and spine and inserting a metal screw for stabilization. The surgeon was amazed that I wasn't paralyzed, and I praised God for that miracle amid the accident's mess.

I was so blessed by Hannity and the whole host of other people who looked out for me during that time. Growing up in foster care, I learned early on that I couldn't trust people's words—I had to look for consistency in their actions. My mom would promise to do better, but then she would revert to old patterns. People would say that they wanted to adopt me but would reject me. It was one thing for someone to say he was there for me, but it was a whole different situation for that person to show up. Hannity didn't just play the part of a friend. He was there for me in action and support.

Other people showed up for me, too. Lara and Eric Trump stayed in contact, sending gifts and well wishes. Donald Trump, Jr., reached out through social media, making sure that I was okay. Dinesh D'Souza and his wife, Debbie, encouraged me and provided wisdom and advice. Diane and Willie Greene took me into their home, caring for me after my surgery and throughout my recovery. There are too many people to list who showed up for me during that time, investing in me and supporting me through that dark time.

God used these people and so many others to show that He was still with me and still working. As I struggled through surgery and the grueling recovery, He brought light into my life through my fans who showered me with support. They cheered me on and brought me joy. A group of foster kids even came to visit me in the hospital and sing songs to me. People showed love and care in the most amazing ways. Gifts and care packages came pouring in, and fans raised money to send me, not taking *no* for an answer. They showed up for me, and this was immensely meaningful.

I eventually got to meet Sean Hannity in person and to thank him for his friendship and support. We sat and shared pizza together, catching up before he extended another generous invitation. He was appearing at an event for Turning Point USA and invited me to briefly speak onstage with him. He told me that I had better say something good, but instead of using the time to share jokes, I took the opportunity to thank him onstage for all that he had done for me.

Instead of stressing on the depressing turn of my circumstances, I focused on what I could change, which was my attitude. I could choose joy and look on the upside. I was alive and not paralyzed. I had fans who loved and supported me, and God had gotten me through difficult times before and would do so again.

As I healed, I tried to make videos, still laughing and carrying on as usual, but it was tough. I wasn't sure what the future held as recovery was a full-time job, but I couldn't change things. So, I didn't stress; I adapted and moved forward. Following Hannity's advice, I focused on healing and recovery. I trusted that God would work out the details that were still too difficult to navigate.

Chapter Twenty

Dreams Fulfilled

Going from a foster house to the White House was an unbelievable experience.

As I healed, I tried to use that time wisely. I was still making videos and was blessed to be learning from positive mentors along the way.

One thing that I have learned in life is that to continue to grow, I need to continually educate myself, learning from mentors who have more experience and wisdom. I focused on doing this while growing my connections and influence.

I never wanted to be someone who didn't go full force after what I wanted. I heard many people say, "I wish that I had done this or that, but I ran out of time." I never wanted to be one of those people. I wanted to accomplish the things that I set out to do. So, even though my accident kept me from working for most of 2019, I made preparations to secure my dreams and my future.

I was disappointed about missing out on the opportunity to go to the White House and meet the president, but I knew that God would lead me in whatever path He wanted me to go. I just needed to keep pushing forward and to be faithful to do what God had called and equipped me to do.

Once again, in God's perfect timing, He made a way to fulfill a dream that I had of meeting the president of the United States of America. As a child, this dream would have been too big to imagine, but God knows the desires of our hearts, and He gives growth to the dreams that He has planted in us.

I got the news that Charlie Kirk, Turning Point USA's founder and director, got me an invitation to the Black Leadership Summit, which featured President Donald J. Trump as a speaker. I was brimming with excitement. This was my second invitation to the White House, and this time, no car accident would stop me. I couldn't believe it.

I was in awe as I walked through the hallowed halls of the White House. I grew up being shuffled from house to house, and now I was in the home of the president of the United States. It was surreal. I had made it from a foster house to the White House. I walked the same halls that many presidents had walked before. I felt as if I were dreaming. I wasn't dreaming, but I was living the American Dream. I had come from nothing to be invited into the grandeur of the greatest home in our Nation's history.

We filed into the East Room of the White House, my eyes passing over the golden drapes and crystal chandeliers, and I couldn't decide if I wanted to pinch myself to see if this was real or pee myself from the nervous energy wracking my body.

President Donald J. Trump got up to speak, putting the room at ease with his confidence and humor. Before I knew it, he began talking about following someone's interactions on Twitter, calling my name to come to the podium. I was shocked to hear my name called, having no idea that the president would be mentioning my name, let along inviting me up to speak. Trembling with excitement, I managed to lower the mic to suit my shorter than Trump stature, words spilling out of my mouth.

"First of all, I just want to say I love President Donald J. Trump." The crowd went wild, applauding in agreement.

I continued, "The media is attacking him, but when they attack him, they are attacking us, because he is out here fighting for us. And they are harassing you, Mr. President," I said, pointing to him. "So they are harassing me," I pointed back to myself. The president patted my shoulder in acknowledgment and respect.

"I want to say one more thing here. A while back, President Trump said when he was talking to a black community, 'If you vote for me, what do you have to lose, because the do-nothing Democrats have done nothing for the black community.' 2020 is around the corner, and we have a lot to lose now because President Donald J. Trump has done so much for the black community. Thank you, President Trump." He shook my hand and gripped me firmly on the shoulder while making eye contact.

The president followed up my remarks by saying, "He's something, and he's a talented, talented guy. And when he started talking," he said, referring to watching one of my Twitter videos, "I watched it once, I watched it twice, and then I called the first lady over said, 'What do you think of this guy?'"

It was amazing that the president of the United States was following me on social media and watching my videos. That meant a lot to me, but what meant even more was the change that President Trump was effecting in the black communities. The Democrats had enslaved black America, stripping away their belief in the American Dream, but Trump was allowing them to rise up. He didn't offer up empty rhetoric—he took decisive action, eliminating regulations that killed jobs, cutting taxes for the middle class, and creating over one million jobs for black Americans. The black unemployment rate plummeted to an all-time low, narrowing the gap between racial disparities in regards to those out of jobs. He replaced handouts with opportunity and the idea that America is great because it is the land of opportunity where anyone can accomplish anything.

Accused of being a racist and bigot, Trump snapped back at the haters by introducing sweeping policy changes that directly impacted the black communities. Creating incentives to stimulate growth and income in underdeveloped communities, Trump brought money to the projects in a way that brought pride to the people instead of the slavery of government handouts.

He reformed the prison policies of Clinton and Biden Era Democrats, which disproportionately targeted black Americans, locking them away and stripping them of opportunity. The American Dream is about opportunity, and President Donald J. Trump set about creating this through the First Step Act, in which prisoners were given chances to be rehabilitated and prepared for a new life beyond their cells. Set free from the shackles of the oppression of the government, these men and women were given the freedom to grow and thrive. Freedom combined with education, Trump allocated more money to historically black colleges and universities (HBCUs) than any previous president.

Is Trump the perfect leader? No. Am I? Definitely not. If my years of Sunday school lessons have taught me anything, it is that God uses imperfect people to do great things. Trump is one of these people. President Obama could have made these changes for our community, but he didn't. Instead, God chose to use a somewhat orange-tinted leader to bring about changes in black America.

Going from a foster house to the White House was an unbelievable experience. Then, to be brought up to the president's podium and introduced by the president himself—God was showing out big time. I couldn't believe it.

When it came time to have an official photo taken with the president, I stood up straight and tall, but he still towered over me. The photographer snapped the picture, and then President Trump said, "You are a great guy, Terrence. Very, very talented."

I am thankful that President Donald J. Trump puts his money where his own motor mouth is. He doesn't offer empty promises, and I respect that. I also recognize that God has called him to do a job, and he is carrying it out to the best of his ability. The world's weight is on his shoulders, and he does what he believes is right, defending the opportunities for us.

If you watch me on social media, it is evident that I agree with President Trump most of the time. However, the beauty of free thought is that I don't have to agree, just as others don't have to always agree with me. Regardless, I pray for the president and want whoever God has chosen to lead to succeed so that our country can excel. When we come together, we can do far more as a nation than when we are divided.

After my very first visit to the White House, I was blessed to be invited back a few more times. One year after my car accident, I was reinvited to the event that I had missed due to the crash. This time, we were invited into the cabinet room for a meeting of African American leaders. Our seats were assigned, and I noticed mine was at the center of the table, to the left of a large chair with no name plaque. *Did this mean that I was seated next to the president of the United States of America?*

President Trump sat down next to me, and I was astounded. How many people have a chance like this in their lifetime? The American Dream was undeniably real, and I was living it.

The president gave a brief introduction and then prompted us to introduce ourselves, working our way around the table. I was up first.

"Well, I am comedian Terrence K. Williams, and I am sitting next to the greatest president since Abraham Lincoln!" I said to loud applause of agreement.

I wanted to say more, but I followed the instructions to introduce myself. As the introductions were spoken around the table, people became more effusive with their praise, speaking for longer and longer periods. I felt disappointed, as if I had missed my opportunity to properly thank the president for all that he had done for our country and me.

After the introductions and discussions by the group, the meeting ended, and we all gathered around the president, laying hands on him in prayer. Prayers were spoken, and God's presence filled the room. It was a once-in-a-lifetime experience that I will treasure forever.

I did finally get a chance to thank President Trump, sharing a quip and a laugh. We were invited up to the Oval Office, taking a picture with him in front of the Resolute Desk, which has been used by presidents since the 1800s.

I said, "Mr. President, can I tell you something real quick?" He looked at me, his eyes squinting, evaluating.

"Mr. President, I ... I just got this new suit, and I don't have to return it because the economy is doing so good." I stuttered slightly, and he looked at me as if were lost in the direction that I was heading.

Regaining my composure, I explained, "Mr. President, I just bought this new suit, and usually I would have to keep the tags on and then return it, but the economy is doing so good that I popped the tags on this one."

It took him a minute, but his face cleared as he understood. He responded, "OK. That's funny. Now, that's funny. For real, that's funny."

The next day, the president retweeted an old video of mine, stating, "We strongly stand with Terrence Williams." It is one thing to support the president, but to know that the president supports me back is the greatest feeling in the world.

It wasn't just about me, though; President Donald J. Trump has consistently shown that he stands for the American Dream and will fight to keep America great. I respect and admire that and will fight alongside anyone working to keep the opportunities provided by the American Dream alive.

If a tiny boy, birthed from the poverty of the projects and a crack-addicted mother, can make it from a foster house to the White House, then the American Dream is real and achievable for everyone.

Epilogue

Part of the Family

"Hey, Terrence, how you doing over there? Are you doing all right?" the president of the United States addressed me directly.

I was a member's guest at a Super Bowl party at Trump International Golf Club when the president spotted me standing on my own. It is a good thing that he is tall, or he never would have seen me over the sea of partygoers.

"Yeah." I was too stunned to make small talk.

He gestured to me, smiling, "Are they taking good care of you?"

I nodded mutely.

"If they can't take care of you, then I don't know who can. Where are you sitting at?" Trump questioned.

"I'm sitting way in the back, Mr. President," my words gradually starting to return.

"No, you aren't. You are sitting right here with us," the president directed.

I was in awe. It was so surreal. *I am dying after this because there was no way to top this. What is next? Nothing else can be this good.*

When the president tells you that you are sitting at his table, you don't question it; you just do it. I know that God is good—God is great, but He was showing out that day.

This kind of thing doesn't happen to a guy like me who grew up in foster care. It was real, and it was true. It was a spur-of-the-moment invitation that I will remember for the rest of my life. The president was so genuine and so kind. He welcomed me to his table, sitting me with his wife and son. I was grinning from ear to ear as I sat with the president, First Lady Melania, and Barron. I could not believe that I would be so welcomed. Say what you will about his politics, but the president did not have to do that, but he did. This speaks volumes about his character.

I am not the only foster child that the president and first lady impacted in a life-altering way. President Donald J. Trump joined forces with first Lady Melania Trump's #BeBest campaign to strengthen America's child welfare system, providing better resources and greater stability to children within the foster care system when they signed an Executive Order on strengthening the Child Welfare System for America's Children.

After about twenty minutes, I initiated the departure from the table. I didn't want to overstay my welcome or intrude on the president's family time.

"Mr. President, I don't want to stay too long, because I know that you need to spend time with your family." I restated, "You need some alone time with your family."

"Oh, come on, man, we are all family here. You are family. We are all family. You can stay however long you want." The president spoke genuinely without a hint of sarcasm or patronizing.

President Donald J. Trump said I'm his family, so I'm his family. Whatever the president says, it goes. So, I'm part of the Trump family now. The president said so. I didn't say so—he said so. I think that he can win the black vote if he adopted me. It would demolish the news cycle with headlines reading, "Trump Adopts Grown Man."

I might not have given away my last name when I was first adopted, but Williams, who? You can call me Terrence K. Trump.